362.2 McCormick, Bob,
MCC   1911-

Facing alcoholism

Date Due

AUG 02 1984	MAR 1 1 1988	7-8-88
AUG 02 1984	MAY 2 4 1989	
NOV 27 1984	APR 1 6 1990	
FEB 19 1985	JUL 2 9 1991	
MAR 12 1985		
DEC 18 1985	MAY 03 1993	
JUN 19 1986	AUG 01 2000	
MAY 13 1987	AUG 06 2008	
DEC 19 1987		
FEB 25 1988		
MAR 1 1 1988		
MAR 1 1 1988		

Facing Alcoholism

Facing Alcoholism

Robert McCormick

Oak Tree Publications, Inc.
San Diego, California

Published by Oak Tree

Copyright © 1982 by Robert McCormick

Distributed in the United States by
Oak Tree Publications, Inc.
San Diego, California

Library of Congress Cataloging in Publication Data

McCormick, Robert, 1911 —
    Facing alcoholism.

    Bibliography: p.
    1. McCormick, Robert, 1911 — . 2. Alcoholics—United
States—Biography. 3. Alcoholism—Treatment. I. Title.
HV5218.M35A34   362.2'9286   81-18678
ISBN 0-916392-83-X   AACR2

First Edition
1 2 3 4 5 6 7 8 9 85 84 83 82
Printed and bound in the United States of America

Contents

Preface

There is hope for the hopeless alcoholic. That is the point I want to make.

Those confronted with an alcoholism problem most often think of four avenues of assistance: a physician, a psychiatrist, a clergyman and Alcoholics Anonymous. The first three are too often a waste of time; the fourth is potentially great but frequently entails overwhelming difficulties. There is a fifth hope for the millions who cannot profit from the big four; that is what motivated me to write this book.

I never had the slightest urge to produce a book. I have been writing for a living all of my adult life and now would far rather devote my time to concentrated loafing. But this subject is different. Like most alcoholics who are again in control of themselves, I care enough to want to help.

The fifth hope is based on no smashing scientific or psychological breakthroughs, no panaceas, no magic potions. It simply involves what are called rehabilitation centers. In a few areas, such centers are well publicized. In others, they are obscure to the point of being invisible.

Readers attempting to make use of the fifth hope (or any of the other four, for that matter) need a far wider and deeper understanding of alcoholism than most people have. I try to contribute to that understanding. The book is based on practical knowledge and endless interviews and conversations, not mounds of data. It is not a preachment or a high-domed venture into amateur psychology or medicine. It is simply an effort to tell people how to meet the problem of alcoholism in a pragmatic way.

Alcoholism is not subject to a quick fix. It is a formless illness, as unpredictable and as varied as the millions of people suffering from it. It causes immeasurable misery, incalculable human and economic waste, and death. Almost anything is worth trying, to fight it.

1

Everybody Gets Into the Act

Almost every family has a drinking problem of some sort and hasn't the faintest idea how to handle it.

The problem may be highly visible or completely concealed; it may be only a worry and annoyance or the direct cause of destructive friction, tragedy, and violence. Its focal point may be an alcoholic husband or wife, a father or mother, a relative, friend, employee, boss, child, or lover. But whoever, wherever it is and no matter how severe, most of us don't know how to get help or what channels for help exist.

This was driven into my heart when I finally was stabilized after my fourth stay in an alcoholic rehabilitation clinic. I had many friends and acquaintances. I was moderately successful and moderately well-known in and from writing, radio, and television. I had long been a reporter-journalist, a profession that once not only accepted but expected heavy drinking.

When word got around that, through some sort of miracle, Bob McCormick was again relatively normal, the telephone calls started. They were mostly pleas for help—and plea is the only word that fits. Some came directly from alcoholics themselves who knew they had to take drastic action; the rest from frantic relatives and colleagues of alcoholics. The ignorance of my friends about alcoholism was as appalling as mine had been.

Getting knowledgeable assistance in trying to recover from alcoholism is difficult, whether the patient is you, your spouse, a relative, a friend, or a valued employee. The most frequently suggested sources of help are a medical doctor, a psychiatrist, a clergyman, or Alcoholics Anonymous. The first three are too often useless. The fourth is invaluable but has limitations.

If there is new hope for alcoholics and their families, it is in the increase in professional alcoholism rehabilitation centers scattered around the country. People generally know almost nothing about these clinics, although there are hundreds, perhaps thousands of them, some good, some bad.

It is such a clinic—a fine one—that the United States Navy runs at Long Beach, California, which has treated such people as Betty Ford, Senator Eugene Talmadge, and Billy Carter. Numerous other prominent and even famous people have gone to other clinics. Former Representative Wilbur Mills is one of the few people of prominence who attributes his renaissance almost entirely to Alcoholics Anonymous, although he, too, went through some treatment before giving himself completely to AA.

Alcoholism is not yet definable as a precise disease. Treatment, in clinics, AA or anywhere else, is uncoordinated. Even the definitions are vague and varied.

Alcoholism, like cancer, can hit anyone. The corporate chairman, who has a man to lay out his clothes and wind his watch, can be just as sodden a mess as the wino who sleeps on a sewer grate. The chairman conceals it more carefully by relying on flunkies who will make the decisions he cannot handle and by sliding into his proto-plasmic state only at home or with tolerant friends. But there is no basic difference in their problems, which are shared by the prostitute who sleeps it off in the women's detention center and the suburban housewife who is found by her children passed out on the kitchen floor.

Just as alcoholism is not a precise disease, neither is its treatment. Some patients may be helped by one or a com-bination of the four better-known sources of help. Too many are not.

Most family doctors know little about alcoholism, do not recognize the disease, have not been trained to handle it, and are not alert to its consequences. When a diseased patient has the courage to ask a doctor for help, he usually will be treated with a pat on the head, an admonition to "cut down on your drinking," and a prescription for a quantity of tranquilizers that can be as dangerous as the original ailment.

Many psychiatrists wisely will not even attempt to treat alcoholics. Perhaps they do not understand al-coholism and consequently cannot cope with it. Perhaps they adhere to the old exhortation that recovery is a matter of willpower, not therapy. Like many physicians, psychia-trists often will dispense prescriptions for tranquilizers or other mind-altering drugs with abandon, often creating an addiction to uppers and downers as a replacement for, or in addition to, an addiction to alcohol.

Clergymen are different. For the most part, they try reason based on religion and conscience. An alcoholic is violating the teachings of his faith, risking divine retribu-tion, when he inflicts the results of his alcoholism on others. His wife leaves him, his children hate him, he loses his job, he loses his home, he wrecks his car, he kills or maims others; he's a slob, and should be ashamed of himself. Such arguments, though sharpened by sincerity and propelled by emotion, seldom penetrate the mind befuddled by excessive use of the most easily obtainable narcotic in the world.

It is safe to postulate that doctors, psychiatrists, and clergymen themselves are not immune to the disease. Among my colleagues at one clinic was a truly distinguished doctor who finally was persuaded to get treatment when he breezed into a hospital early one morning and asked a head nurse at what time he was scheduled to perform a particularly delicate operation. He could not mask his surprise and discomfort when he was told he had successfully performed the surgery the morning before. He had been in a drunken blackout. Incidentally, he was cross-addicted to drugs as well as alcohol.

At another clinic, my group included a reputable and expensive psychiatrist who also was cross-addicted and subject to total blackouts. And one of my "classes" at a clinic included a nun, a lay brother of the Catholic Church, two priests, a monsignor, and perhaps six or seven Protestant clergymen.

These scattered facts are not, in themselves, condemnatory of the medical or psychiatric professions, or of any church. They do dramatize the theory that the pursuance of these professions does not routinely qualify a person to treat the disease of alcoholism.

Thus, Alcoholics Anonymous might seem the only place left for the alcoholic to go, assuming he has sufficient wit left to conclude that he needs help. AA, to one who knows it, is one of the greatest organizations in the world; its Twelve Steps are masterful in wording, in scope, and in understanding. Its group therapy is sometimes miraculous. But a sizable portion of people who need or want help either reject AA without trying it, or are repelled when they do try it. They are turned off—sometimes by the religious overtones, sometimes by the very idea of admitting to themselves and others that they are alcoholics, sometimes by the excuse that the meeting room is too cold or the man sitting behind them ate onions at dinner.

Even the fifth alternative—the alcoholic rehabilitation center—is far from infallible. The "cure" rate, a deceptive description to begin with, probably is no better than 60 to 80 percent at the best clinics. Yet the clinic affords the most concentrated, presumably the most skillful treatment now known, bringing together professionals who specialize in alcoholism. Generally, it gets the toughest cases. Many of its patients have been through other clinics without success. Some have been sentenced by courts to take treatment or are under mandate from welfare agencies. While others are sent by their bosses or families with ultimatums to straighten out or get lost.

The clinic can be the first resort, rather than the last. After a course at one of the better centers, the most recalcitrant patient may well be more receptive to AA, or to a psychiatrist, a doctor, or a clergyman, if he can find one who talks his language. Under any circumstance, the clinic is worth a try.

The first rehabilitation center in which I served time was recommended to me—urged upon me—by a very well-known member of the U.S. Congress, on whom it had worked wondrously. He was only the first, and perhaps not the most interesting, in an amazing cast of characters I was to meet. Everybody, it seemed, was getting into the act. At my first group therapy session, for example, a dozen people sat around an austere but pleasant room, propped at varying angles in folding chairs. There were eight men, three women and one teenager, a girl of 16. Their backgrounds included:

—A steel worker who had stabbed his wife 23 times but so botched the job that she lived.

—A senior vice president of a big and powerful New

York bank whose fiscal activities had become confused.

—An adroit pianist who was director of music for the public school system of one of our more populous states.

—A Southern farm wife with several convictions for prostitution who said matter-of-factly that she had experienced incestuous relations with her father since she was 12, and enjoyed them.

—A bearded young fellow whose hobby was beating his wife.

—A brilliant youth who celebrated too enthusiastically when Saul Bellow won the Nobel Prize.

—A middle-aged government worker who carried a pistol for weeks in search of his nagging, unfaithful, and estranged wife.

—The spouse of a high-ranking Naval officer who had totaled several cars in a string of automobile accidents and otherwise endangered her husband's career, her own life, and the lives of her three children.

—A male schoolteacher who had practiced his gay proclivities once too often on a very young boy.

—The head of a regional automobile distributorship, who had gradually ceased heading and ceased distributing.

—A nun, pretty and placid in appearance, whose only transgressions had been against the rules of her church.

—A 16-year-old girl who stole several thousand dollars from her mother, ran away, and eventually was picked up by police with a group of rioting gays from whom she had received comfort and protection.

So it went, in four other similar rooms in two different buildings in a bucolic setting of pastureland and trees. Sixty-five people with only one thing in common: they were lucky enough to be in a place where they could get expert help and treatment for the consuming, widespread, indiscriminate disease of alcoholism. There are hundreds of alcoholic rehabilitation centers scattered around the country. Called by different names, they are relatively unknown by any name.

I entered the first one more or less voluntarily, not counting heavy pressure from my wife. I came out in the best shape I had been for years, physically and mentally. For about a month I gave my wife Peggy a happy flashback of the man she had married. Then she died, and my life collapsed. Her death did, however, give me the excuse I needed to resume my drinking. Who could blame me? When I had retired from NBC a few months earlier, I had become even more dependent upon Peggy than I had been before—dependent intellectually and spiritually, although she had been desperately sick for years with emphysema. Having gone through such double-trouble, such intense and prolonged trauma, it was only natural that I would disintegrate. At least, that's the way I figured it. I took a trip to Samoa, a spot I liked, where for a time my drinking would not be interrupted by daily chores and the necessity of maintaining a facade.

When I returned a month or so later, I spent three weeks in a hospital intensive care unit with what was ominously called "congestive heart failure." The next development I can remember, I was in another alcoholic rehabilitation center. I somehow walked out—and bam! I wound up in still another. After a few days, I got out of that one, too.

Those episodes, I was convinced, were abductions. The kidnappings consisted mostly of taking me by the hand, leading me to a car, then to an alcoholic ward and to a bed. It required all the physical effort of taking a large oyster out of a stew.

All this was done by two gentle, kindly, and savvy neighbors. They were responsible for getting me into the

fourth "drunk tank," as we veteran sober alcoholics sometimes refer to them. Why they bothered, I will never understand. They were too young and too busy to work on
lost causes.

I disliked the fourth clinic, and the people who ran it
reciprocated generously. But something happened during
that period. I straightened out, and I knew it. I stayed the
stipulated 28 days, but the management didn't think I was
fit to turn loose. They insisted I stay longer, which I was
convinced would harm me irreparably. Then, they decided I was hopeless anyhow, and, in effect, threw me
out. I haven't had a drink since and I don't want a drink
and I don't even think about a drink. I don't mind being
around booze, I don't mind others drinking, and I serve it
in my home.

Four years went by before I found out I was not
kidnapped for the fourth go-round. My neighbors had
made excellent but fruitless arguments to try to persuade
me to accept treatment again. They tell me that I actually
phoned them and agreed. Where this flash of common
sense came from is utterly beyond me. I have no recollection of it, but I'm awfully glad it happened.

2

Who's a Drunk?

Probably the most difficult problem with any alcoholic is getting him to realize and admit he is an alcoholic. Before anything good can happen, he must not only say he is a drunk—he must believe it. Only then can he be helped.

What constitutes an alcoholic? No definitive tests exist, as yet, and there are almost as many definitions as there are alcoholics. Alcoholics Anonymous wisely sums it up by saying, in effect:

you are an alcoholic when you are powerless over alcohol and when booze has made your life unmanageable.

The more that rule is studied, the better it is understood, the wiser it seems. Life does not become obviously unmanageable for all alcoholics. Some will continue to get away with it, perhaps for years, perhaps until it is too late. And many alcoholics find it impossible to concede they are powerless over alcohol when they can occasionally go for days, weeks, or months without a drink—or when they kid themselves into truly believing they only have a couple of belts at bedtime to help them sleep or loosen their libidos. Yet even the binge drinker, who blows up periodically but otherwise stays as dry as a mesa top, can be an alcoholic. So can that common suburban phenomenon, the weekend martini man, or the weekend beer drinker. Or the person who sanctimoniously drinks only white wine—but in quantity.

If the AA definition has a flaw, therefore, it lies in the fact that it may be too generalized. It covers so much, that we may not recognize ourselves as meeting the qualifications.

Alcoholics do not want to recognize themselves; that is axiomatic. I didn't. My wife Peggy tried patiently and valiantly to make me understand, but I had lied to myself so effectively that I thought she was lying. Or imagining, or distorting. I am particularly bitter about my own perfidiousness (to myself). If my thinking had been less scrambled, I would have subjected myself to treatment sooner than I did and saved everybody, including myself, much unnecessary torment.

We can have the same difficulties identifying others as alcohol addicts. Married people have tolerated idiosyncratic behavior by their spouses for years without suspecting such aberrations were syndromes of alcoholism. Close relatives go undetected, as do friends, employees, bosses, sons, daughters—anyone—because few people know how to distinguish a true alcoholic from what is known as a social drinker, a controlled drinker. Only a small percentage of alcoholics are skid row bums. Many can qualify outwardly as community leaders, fine family figures, successful job holders. There are, however, vivid and detailed behavioral patterns that distinguish the two. The patterns do not constitute proof, but they can be considered convincing evidence. If they are to assist in treatment, both the subject and those around him should be cognizant of signs of the disease. This is possible only through an awareness of some of the distinguishing marks of an alcoholic.

One of the more reliable signs is a dependence on alcohol to help slide through anything resembling an exacting situation. You have a 10 A.M. meeting, for example, at which you must sign a number of legal papers and a bank check or two. But you have that routine difficulty, the shakes, and your signature, when you can manage it at all, looks like a one-dimensional pile of spilled toothpicks. A couple of hefty belts, as a rule, will enable you to squeak out something that will suffice and might even be legible.

Without the after-burner kick supplied by the emergency booze, you or I may have a lack of self-confidence that approaches fright. We will try to delay or avoid even the simplest task. Even now, I sometimes must flagellate myself to call the plumber, buy a pair of shoes, call stores for prices on products, or perform some other fundamental function that most people consider routine.

Disintegration frequently becomes evident in late afternoon—before leaving work, before the children get home from school, or sometimes after home is reached. Workers with irregular hours, of course, have varying schedules. Whatever times their craving clocks are set for, the metabolic patterns can be completely blown apart by a disruption such as a long airplane trip—a confusion they often solve by drinking from takeoff to landing, ending up with jet sag as well as lag.

Some drinkers depend upon alcohol to get their work done, whether they be judges or ditchdiggers. Some depend on it to sleep, others to wake up. Some feel liquor is essential to the celebration of a holiday or the signing of a money-laden contract; some feel it just as essential to smooth over loneliness on a holiday or to mourn the loss of a money-laden contract. Some feel it will alleviate despondency, and, by the same token, afford a proper release for happiness.

One of the most common justifications for drinking is the plaintive statement, "I've got to have a couple of jolts to calm my nerves." In some form, it is used after a turbulent day at the office, in the kitchen, on the freeway, or any other time an alcoholic thinks he will be believed if he contends he has been through unreasonable tension and turmoil. It is particularly useful after a tax audit, the death of a friend or a pet, or after a family fight.

I knew a young and attractive housewife who had to snort four or five ounces before she had the courage to drive a familiar route downtown. A well-known industrialist had to go through the same ceremony before leaving for a three-Manhattan lunch with his peers.

Similar routines had to be followed by a middle-aged pinstripe-suiter before he started an air trip, which was at least twice weekly, and by a master carpenter before and during relatively simple hammer-and-saw jobs. There was the skillful and nice golfer who had to have periodic bottle-warmth preceding and in the course of an exhibition or a match. And the radio-and-television "personality," and the commercial pilot, and the foreman on a moving van, and the tinsmith. It goes on and on.

Total dependence on alcohol can be a matter of what time it is, as well as what lies ahead. Some of my best friends cannot start the morning without priming themselves with vodka. Some begin getting fidgety in mid-morning and regain their composure only after a wet lunch.

Marital and job problems are especially popular alibis. Husbands, wives, children, bosses, and co-workers are given credit for driving thousands of alcoholics to drink. It becomes a circular wind pattern of paranoia; the more the alcoholic uses these handy covers for drinking, the more he drinks and the greater the blame he lays off on his spouse or boss or whoever is nearby, the more obnoxious he becomes and the more he thinks he is being abused. It's obviously endless.

Pain and discomfort also are well-used excuses. The suffering can be real or imaginary; a tooth extraction is very reliable. "The Flu," whatever it may actually be, does double duty. It can serve both as a provocation for drinking and as a camouflage for a hangover.

There are the nervous types who become extremely jittery, irritable or sullen when they cannot get their opiate. They may pace the floor, insist on "doing something," or "going somewhere." If they are ingenious, they will think of a reason to run an errand that can include a bar stop or an impromptu visit with a sympathetic friend or at any other place they can manipulate a drink.

The active alcoholic cannot fight off a drink when it is available, either at a party or in the privacy of his own bedroom. At a party, he may go through all sorts of gyrations to conceal the fact that he is filching drinks or, less likely, he may take "just one" for the sake of camaraderie. This can lead to use of the time-worn cliché, "I was with Joe last night, and did *he* get me bombed." "He" didn't get anybody bombed, except perhaps himself. The victim did the job. He didn't need help.

What is important about all this is not the situations involved, but the fact that the principals cannot resist or *must have* alcohol, if there is a difference. The situations are simply excuses, not reasons. The sometimes unbearable distress of needing or wanting a drink, whether regularly or sporadically, distinguishes alcoholics. Perhaps the only significant difference between the respectable librarian who rushes to the nearest saloon at quitting time and the unshaven bum is that the latter doesn't need an excuse. He lives to drink, but the librarian must rationalize his or her action, to self and others.

Not all alcoholics inevitably wind up each day limp and soggy, but they come close and achieve it more often as the body's tolerance declines.

And decline the tolerance does, sooner or later. For a time, the liver builds up mechanisms to handle the alcohol flood, but eventually, it reaches a point of exhaustion.

Studies have indicated that the drinker's tolerance follows a regular, predictable pattern whether he keeps drinking or not. First, the tolerance level will rise, may get pretty high and allow the possessor to brag about drinking everybody else under the table. Then at some point it will drop rather precipitously. If, at any point on the tolerance line, the drinker knocks it off for a time—perhaps a month or a year or so—then resumes, his tolerance will build back up quickly at the level it would have been if he had kept on drinking. I suppose there is an explanation for this phenomenon, but if I've heard it, I haven't understood it.

The progression from rising tolerance to no tolerance is natural. Related to dependence on alcohol is the inability to shut the intake valve once it is opened. It is standard procedure for a loyal alcoholic to want just a couple of strands of the "hair of the dog" to cure a hangover; it is also standard for the alcoholic thus to accumulate another hangover.

The "wee nip" remedy for a hangover—or to warm up or to relax or to forget—too often ends only when the booze is all gone or the nipper is a gelatinous blob. The need for the first drink may be pressing, or it may simply seem a pleasant idea; the need for the second drink is usually real, to accomplish what the first drink did not quite manage. The third slug is both needed, and enticing. From that point, it is a greased pole. Men and women participate equally. Examples of such performances are common everywhere, even during quiet evenings at home. Whatever the details, if it happens consistently the odds are that the principal is an alcoholic.

An intriguing aspect of these behavioral patterns is that the drunk knows he has them but he lies about them—not only to others but to himself. And he believes his own lies. I did. Only a handful of other people realized what I knew but would not face—that my dependence upon alcohol was complete. When confronted with the facts, I would solemnly deny them and I was perfectly sincere. It's a state of mind that is, I suppose, another example of alcoholic insanity. A drink would usually wipe out any guilt I might have felt about deceiving myself.

The binge drinker also can be an alcoholic; only his timing is different. The person who insists he is not an alcoholic because only once or twice a year does he go on a real honker can be addicted to those explosions. He probably cannot be classified as an alcoholic if he takes one of his trips on the spur of the moment, and with real justification—a truly gala or shattering event. But if his desire to get drunk builds up over a period of time, and the tension of resisting increases proportionately until he finally can resist no longer, he is most likely an alcoholic. The outbursts don't have to be at regular intervals; Mount St. Helens' eruptions are irregular and her periods of quiescence are extended, but she is still an active volcano.

The alcoholic's need for a drink—it can be more than a craving, it can be a truly desperate, painful necessity— can lead him into brilliant maneuvers to insure the continuity of his supply. I knew one man who bought a beautiful ancient brass bedstead because the four corner posters had removable tops and each neatly held a fifth of gin. He got the idea from a old Sid Caesar television skit called, I believe, "The Drunkard."

The innovative skill of the drunk fearing drought is magnificent. The fear probably comes most often from overt family antagonism. A wife, husband, or alert child may well be the first to sense the alcoholism and be taking clumsy steps to handle it. But it can also rest on the dread of being exposed as a heavy drinker, although the drinker himself very likely has convinced himself he is doing nothing wrong or unusual; family or friends or bosses or co-workers who might object simply aren't understanding. But whatever the reason, the predicament can result in great creative ploys to sneak drinks, enabling the drinker to declare righteously that he "had only a couple of beers at lunch."

One of my early idols was a close relative who lived with his very old mother. His mother could not tolerate hard liquor but did not object to blackberry or elderberry wine, preferably homemade. She even allowed rice wine. She had some herself, several times a day. Anyhow, my kin had a cabinet-type humidifier in his bedroom, which he kept going constantly, even during Washington's sultriest summers. His mother did not know the cabinet contained no humidifier, just a noisy electric motor that camouflaged a small jerry-built still, which each day transformed a panful of homemade rice wine into straight alcohol of about 160 or 180 proof. That was enough, on top of what was consumed at bars during the day, to send my beloved kin to bed thoroughly sloshed night after night.

Other more common examples:

The man or woman who keeps a bottle stashed in the car trunk, preferably under trash, and who stops in uncrowded or inconspicuous spots for a few large gulps. This device is a favorite with husbands whose wives mark the levels of booze in open bottles, or who confiscate any liquor they find around the house.

The man or woman who finds hiding places inside the house. A man with a cluttered workroom has a lovely setup. Pints can rest on top of the furnace ducts, or in air vents or under the circular saw or at the bottom of the big wastebasket, or any one of a hundred other places.

The woman can utilize the sewing basket, the dirty clothes hamper, the big pot that holds the Norfolk pine, the toilet, an empty vinegar bottle, the underside of a cushion on a seldom-used chair, the bottom of the flour canister, the back of a kitchen cabinet, an antique covered soup tureen used only for special dinners.

Outdoors, of course, the possibilities are limited only by the imagination. Reachable roof gutters are very handy, as are loose patio flagstones and areas where garden supplies are stored, and any cluttered storage spaces. The same ranges of possibilities are available in offices and other working areas.

At one time or another, I used many of these hiding places, plus others, but my favorite was pragmatically fitted to my own requirements. Stopping at a bar after work took too much time and money, so I secreted pints or half-pints in my car. As I got near home, I would stop at preselected deserted roadside spots and take several enormous blasts from a bottle. I tried to gauge the ritual so I wouldn't get too drunk, or pass out, until I was safely inside the house. Sometimes I made it. Sometimes not.

Most systems of maintaining alcoholic irrigation have drawbacks. One of the more bothersome is disposal of the empties, be they bottles or cans. They can be dumped stealthily into a neighbor's trash or public receptacles. They can be left in laundry rooms, or buses, or in back alleys. One entrepreneur bought a glass-cutting gadget with which, according to the advertisements, he could convert used bottles into vases, glasses, and lamps. To explain the sudden accumulation of dead soldiers in the basement, he told his wife he was collecting them from friends. But though he worked assiduously, he got farther and farther behind; in addition, skinny pints and drab quart gin bottles made atrocious vases, glasses, and lamps, and the plan fell apart.

Anyone who can get liquor in miniature bottles has an advantage. They fit in pockets and purses with a minimum of bulges and can be tossed away more readily. Overcoats are particularly useful; the pockets hold several of the little jugs and tend to cushion them against rattling.

Sometimes the worries begin with the purchasing of booze, rather than what to do with the empties. Particularly in a small town or a tight intimate neighborhood, word gets around that Mr. Smith is buying an astonishing amount at the local liquor store since his household is supposedly temperate, if not abstemious. So the buyer may have to go to a different liquor store each day, if he can. Or he may have to ask friends, or office boys, or sometimes even total strangers to get what he needs. It can be a nuisance and an embarrassment.

These peculiar behavioral traits do not constitute a definition of an alcoholic, but they are a tiny cross section of some of the symptoms. There are many others, some of which must be judged on how often they occur and with what intensity.

Almost all of us can recognize the slurred speech, the wobbly legs, the sway from the hips, the tendency to knock over cups, the uncoordinated eyeballs. But even when these signs are not obvious, there are others, such as tedious repetition; words, phrases, sentences, and even long arguments delivered over and over again. They become particularly deadly when they don't make much sense the first time.

Then, of course, there is the person who becomes bellicose or amorous; chances are he couldn't back up either mood with any appreciable physical substance.

Harder to spot is one of the most positive evidences of alcoholism, or, for that matter the excessive use of both hard and soft drugs (if there is a distinction). That elusive factor is the blackout. Periods ranging from minutes to weeks can be totally obliterated from a drugged mind. Not a shred of memory of the blackout period exists even under hypnosis.

In some cases, of course, events can be reconstructed. A first-rate journalist friend learned to fly when he was in his late thirties. He bought his own plane, was considered a good pilot, flew himself and friends all over the West for fun and relaxation. Booze was an integral part of most trips. Then one noon my friend woke up in a Las Vegas hotel but had no recollection whatever of getting there. He had, he learned, flown his own plane down from San Francisco the night before, stone drunk and in a blackout. He quit flying.

At gatherings of honest alcoholics, in clinics and elsewhere, you can hear innumerable stories about automobile accidents of which the prime figure remembers zilch. A thirty-second blackout descended without warning and the result is a twisted mass of wreckage and, too often, bodies. Immediately before the accident and immediately after, the driver, although under the influence, might seem quite capable of handling a car.

Businessmen tell of settling deals, hiring people, making appointments, promising action, and otherwise reaching decisions while articulate but mentally unconscious. Housewives describe burned roasts, overfilled bathtubs, unkept dinner dates, unpaid or twice-paid bills, unentered checks, and miscellaneous other goofs.

One young fellow had a wild, orgiastic night with a

woman other than the mother of his two children. When he somehow stumbled home the next morning, he lost his wife because his disheveled appearance painfully showed what he had been doing during his unexplained absence, and he lost his new-found girlfriend because he could remember absolutely nothing of what pleasures he'd had, or even where he had been.

As a matter of fact, the steel worker who had stabbed his wife 23 times on a Friday night didn't know it until he was told by the jail warden the following Monday.

The moral of all this is take heed—when someone says, "Of course you knew George died; I told you over the phone two days after it happened"; or "What do you mean, you weren't invited? I came by your place last Tuesday just to ask you"; or "Well, I gave you my new address twice and you wrote it down both times," the alcoholic is moving toward serious trouble.

The list of ways in which alcoholism betrays itself is interminable, and this random summary is intended only to be helpful to the drinker assessing himself and to those around him who really care. It is not in any way to be considered ridicule of the alcoholic; alcoholism isn't funny, any more than the hesitant walk of a stroke survivor, or the twitches of a spastic or the scars of a burn victim. Alcoholism is a killer disease and the more quickly it can be recognized, the better the chance for successful treatment. But to be recognized, it must be understood.

3

Alcoholic Thinking or Non-thinking...

A devoted alcoholic can rarely think clearly, with or without a drink. He thinks he can think and that is his first aberration. He will proclaim loudly that his mind is clear as a bell. But what a bell! Made of goose feathers and wet wood. He may seem to be functioning, but his behavior often is weird, his judgment frightful, his intellectual confusion exasperating. And the condition may recur sporadically for weeks, months, even years after he last had a drink. It may even be permanent.

Alcoholic thinking is an elusive matter. We know it is there just as we know when there is a strange smell in the room. But trying to grab it for careful examination is difficult. To make alcoholic thinking at all understandable, we must first be aware of the process of treating alcoholism—at least the process I believe is most widely accepted as standard.

Quitting booze roughly involves three overlapping stages. First is drying out—detoxifying—filtering out the alcohol in the blood. It has no more lasting effect than a laxative and, with proper medication to head off delirium tremens and convulsions, is perhaps the easiest part. It usually takes from five to eight days.

Then comes sobering up, the process of learning to operate without alcohol and trying to learn to resist alcohol. For this, the customary allocation is about twenty-eight days.

The third phase is a period of stabilization and maintenance, the achievement of true sobriety in which neither alcohol nor alcoholic thinking is a factor. There are, of course, variations and exceptions in the pattern, as there are about anything connected with the use of drugs. But the more experienced experts, including therapists and followers of Alcoholics Anonymous, seldom refer to a drunk as cured or recovered. He is always "recovering." Once an alcoholic, always an alcoholic. I have not, at this point, had a drink for years, but I am "recovering" and I never take for granted that I am safe. I have known numerous addicts who got by nicely for nine years, or fifteen or twenty, then blew it. Perhaps the prize among my friends is one of the finest, most brilliant, most self-disciplined and most successful men I have ever known who was drinkless for thirty-seven years. Then, without discernible cause or warning, he skidded clear off the road. After several months, he pulled himself out of the ditch and has been straight ever since, a period of several years. At his age, after another thirty-seven years he will have it made.

THE REAL YOU?

Among many misconceptions about the alcoholic is the ancient theory that the true self is disclosed when drunk, that a few slugs bring out the real you; if you beat your children, set the house on fire, get into unprovoked fights, end up in jail, or abruptly take off for a whorehouse, it's because that is what you've always wanted to do but haven't dared. The theory for the most part is poppycock. Some inhibitions will be lowered when drunk, but also the alcoholic can be nuts. When alcoholic thinking takes over, you are just plain crazy.

Typically, the drunk whether soaked or recently dried-out, is convinced that he is a good husband and father, even when his wife is about to leave him, his children loath him or are ashamed of him, and other relatives avoid him. He thinks he is a surgically sharp businessman though he has an unblemished record of bungling. He thinks he's an outstanding worker though his bosses, colleagues, and performance records don't bear him out. He thinks he drives perfectly well when drunk, though he knows half the people in traffic court by their first names. He thinks he has close and faithful friends, though all are mere drinking buddies who will desert him forthwith if either side is sober. He thinks he is entertaining, clever, and erudite though his associates find him boring and ludicrous.

He may go into unprovoked fits of laughter or sulks or rages, producing child abuse, battered wives, and angry neighbors. He thinks he is persecuted; anything that goes wrong is somebody else's fault. He procrastinates and when he does act, he says and does the wrong things. He takes goofy positions in arguments, is dogmatic about things of which he knows little or nothing. He is hypercritical of others but has no capacity to criticize himself, except when in a penitent mood, and then any self-assessment will be maudlin, shallow and temporary. He is often slovenly except when he tries to conceal his drinking by being too suave, too carefully dressed, too well manicured and barbered. He is arrogant or servile to extremes; he thinks no woman can resist him or, conversely, no woman can abide him.

It goes on and on and on. Alcoholic thinking covers an enormous area and is one of the least understood manifestations of too much too often. It appears most frequently in the genuine alcoholic, but it is not unknown among the heavy social drinker.

The drunk himself usually cannot and will not discuss the problem; he becomes livid at the idea that he does not make sense, that he is an alcoholic or even that he drinks too much. In a crisis, such as the threat of losing his job or family, he may promise to quit but he won't. He has great difficulty talking to anyone about personal problems, because the conversation almost inevitably gets around to his drinking, which he will not confront. Thus the endless cartoons of the sodden drunk chewing the bartender's ear; he is fairly certain the bartender won't make him uncomfortable.

PERMANENT BRAIN DAMAGE

The most disturbing feature of alcholic thinking is the fact that it often—usually—does not end when the drinking ends. It can persist for years. Brain damage can be permanent, as has been found in autopsies. The process of alcoholic thinking by a dry person is sometimes referred to as a "dry drunk," a phrase that is not, to me, descriptive or meaningful. But post-drinking idiocy is difficult to define. To me, the condition was best demonstrated by a story attributed to the time of Louis XIV of France. I don't mean to imply that Marie Antoinette was a barfly, but she could have been echoing the logic of any drunk with the legendary line "Let 'em eat cake."

The phenomenon of alcoholic thinking was particularly impressed upon me during my long and close relationships with some of the country's top politicians. I have a much higher regard for the professional politician than do many of my colleagues and most of the public, which is why I was saddened when I saw one buried by the debris of assinine commitments made during spurts of alcoholic thinking. Jobs would be promised to people no more qualified than my French poodle; federal funding would be guaranteed for projects that even the most faithful constituents would find repulsive; theater seats in the President's private box would be promised when the politician didn't know whether the President had a reserved box, and didn't really have any influence at the White House anyhow.

Grander matters could be at issue—corporate mergers, for example, that involved tens of millions of dollars or that might run into overwhelming Wall Street opposition and entanglement with anti-trust laws or powerful federal regulatory agencies. Or log-rolling on crucial legislation: yes, I'll vote for your bill if you will vote for mine; a smidgeon of sober thought would have reminded the log-roller that his political career would be ended summarily if he voted for the other man's legislation.

In business, also, the possible consequences could be frightening, as when a despotic board chairman insisted on selling off parts of his conglomerate though it would have destroyed him and his empire.

These bizarre occurrences, and countless others, came even after the principals had been dried out and had reached presumed sobriety. When an alcoholic is able to recognize alcoholic thinking and when he can deal with it before he makes a sometimes tragic jackass of himself, he can be considered truly stabilized. His addiction may still be there. But it is under control.

In practical terms, these prolonged intellectual hangovers that afflicted most true alcoholics give a hollow sound to protestations that "I'm sober as a camel; I haven't had a drink all day." Or all week, or all month. The fact that a man or woman is dry does not mean that he or she is at peak efficiency and wisdom, whether he be an editor, a Hollywood stunt man, an actor, a broadcaster, or a bos'ns mate. In situations that long experience have made routine, the dry alcoholic may do just fine. But in an extraordinary crisis involving decisions without precedents and with no standardized procedures, he can disintegrate.

I will never forget nor forgive my own slow-witted reaction during one of my dry periods when, as boss of a portion of the news department, I got an emergency message at lunch that several Puerto Ricans were trying to shoot up Blair House where President Truman was staying while the White House was being repaired. I decided to ignore the whole thing; it was, I solemnly decided, just some demonstrators in a routine disturbance with White House police. Fortunately, I was saved by my staff people who wisely acted on their own.

The lingering, lurking aspects of alcoholic fuzziness are difficult to handle. Commercial airlines around the world theoretically have regulations that crew members cannot drink for 24 to 48 hours before a flight. Some countries, notably Sweden, have strict laws and severe penalties to discourage driving a car for a specified time after having even one snort. But no such black-and-white, statistical standards can guarantee that a brain is working properly.

So it is that an alcoholic cannot be relied upon just because, for the moment, he could pass a breatholator test. It also accounts for the growing popularity in courts of the defense plea "I am an alcoholic and didn't know what I was doing," a defense used in everything from vandalism to such big-time operations as Abscam, where the FBI caught several members of Congress allegedly willing to accept bribes from phony Arab sheiks. Few would argue that such a plea should be a surefire defense, but perhaps it should be given the same weight as a plea of insanity. That's what it is.

4

I Can Quit Any Time
I Want To

A scientifically balanced poll undoubtedly would be impossible, but it certainly is a fact that practically all untreated drunks insist they could knock off the booze any time they want to. Literally that may be true. The code words are "any time I want to."

Drinking is fun up to a point. For the heavy drinker it is often bliss. The joys so vary with individuals, that they cannot be itemized. Alcohol can give you the courage to tell your boss where he can stuff your job, or to make a pass at your best friend's wife, or to head for the airport on impulse and hop a plane for Anchorage to see your old friend Harry. It can let you dance on the piano, or laugh enthusiastically at things that aren't funny, or tell your favorite story about the one-legged waiter. At the other extreme, the greatest pleasure can consist of being just a half-conscious, incoherent blob.

A surprising number of "recovering" as well as active alcoholics take delight in reminiscing about how they went to sleep on the lawn on a winter's night, thinking they were tucked in bed. Or how they spent a night in jail or passed out at their desks, or jumped rope on the ledge around the roof of a ten-story apartment building, or started a hopeless fight with cops summoned by the neighbors to calm down the party.

True, these pleasures are tempered by anguish, guilt, and embarrassment, for obvious reasons; there are also physical effects, which combine with the others to produce pain—genuine physical and mental pain. But these can be eased by one drink.

So the drunk who maintains firmly he can quit any time he wants to, probably believes it. In one sense, he wants to quit, but not enough to give up what he considers the fun. He would like to dump the problems but not the pleasures. Drunken escapades are the high points of some peoples' lives. And most drunks are afraid to stop because they cannot conceive of living without their magic escapes and their emotional props. They think it would be a life of unmitigated horror.

In addition, after a period of drinking, sometimes short, sometimes extended, they have probably built up an addiction, psychological if not physical; withdrawal alone can be messy. When the pain of drinking is greater than the pleasure, the alcoholic is most receptive to treatment. He has hit bottom, as the professionals say. He can go only up—or out.

The location of "bottom" varies with different people. Sometimes it is regarded as reached when an alcoholic loses his job or his family, or when he is in serious trouble with the police or with local, state or federal officials, such as tax collectors. Certainly bottom has been reached when all three happen, if alcohol contributed to his difficulties and if he still doesn't stop drinking. The only lower point comes when the alcoholic is a derelict panhandler, the last stop before social and perhaps physical extinction. Or, to quote the first step of Alcoholics Anonymous' Twelve

Steps to Sobriety: "We admitted we were powerless over alcohol—that our lives had become unmanageable."

The drunk's conviction that he can quit any time is probably based largely on ego or shame. He may honestly think he has the courage, willpower, and that mysterious attribute called "character" which he considers necessary to quit drinking. Or he is ashamed that he doesn't. That is one reason the idea that alcoholism is a disease, not a question of mind over matter, is emphasized during treatment.

Probably most alcoholics have tried to quit. Some succeed for brief periods. I always conceded it would be virtually impossible for me to quit smoking, so I never tried, but I quit drinking hundreds of times. Rarely would my resolve last weeks or months; usually it dissipated in minutes. So common is the phenomenon that it is the subject of numerous short films shown at rehabilitation centers and is heavily emphasized at AA meetings. In truth the overwhelming majority of alcoholics cannot quit without help and conditioning.

One type of I-can-quitter is the "I'll never touch another drop." He usually has had a mighty bad time immediately preceding his renunciation; he usually has made a horse's patoot of himself, perhaps seriously damaged himself or others. If his crisis, repentence, and hangover are sufficiently rough, his heartfelt reformation may last a few days. Then comes the inevitable thought process of "oh, what the hell, one little glass of wine (or one martini or one beer) can't hurt" and he's off again.

Those in this classification really mean what they say about quitting at the moment they say it and may do so, until the desire for a drink overwhelms the desire to stay dry. It is not necessarily an act, not an attempt to mollify those who are angry or disgusted with them. It's sincere. It just doesn't last very long, once the hangover passes.

Another type of quitter will decide to taper off or put restrictions on himself that will make him an acceptable social drinker, a controlled drinker who will never again allow himself to go berserk.

He may decide never to have a drink at lunch, or none before dinner, or none after dinner, or none when alone. He may never have a drink at a party or may never have a drink except at a party. He may decide to drink only wine or only beer or only vanilla extract. What he sturdily refuses to recognize is the fact that all the substitutes contain alcohol and all ultimately have the same effect as 120-proof rum. The drinker can and does get just as drunk and sooner or later, he's back in his old routine.

Another futile procedure involves limiting one's drinks to one or two or however many a day. It requires unremitting exercise of self-discipline and prolongs the agony of quitting. The practitioner is constantly reminded of what he's missing. It is probably the hardest route to sobriety.

A common variety of renunciator sets deadlines for himself. The drinker who gives it up for Lent or while his wife is pregnant or while his driver's license is suspended probably never even pretends he will make it permanent. Such deadline setting is one of the worst approaches anyhow. The person who makes bets with friends that he can go a stipulated time without booze is simply setting himself a time at which he can cut loose. Also, it is easy to cheat and soothe guilt by rationalizing that the four drinks he had with the boss didn't count because his promotion might have been in the balance, or those he had on his wedding anniversary were essential because his marriage might have been jeopardized.

Alcoholics Anonymous recommends a type of deadline setting, but it is different. It is embodied in the famous slogan: "One Day at a Time." It's a continuing pledge rather than a deadline; it means simply that the person promises himself he will not take that first drink *today*, and it goes on day after day. I have known recovering alcoholics who actually set their time limits at ten or twenty minutes; their cravings were on such hair triggers that they continually had to remind themselves to leave the booze alone.

Controlled drinking—social drinking—is the ambition of practically all drunks, even a few of the skid row alcove-sleepers. It is also practically impossible for an alcoholic. The results of presumably learned studies will appear periodically implying it is possible for a lush to become a sipper, but on very careful reading the studies apply the possibility not to true alcoholics but to nonaddicted heavy drinkers. They confine the hope for moderation to such small groups that statistically and realistically they mean almost nothing. And in some instances, honest studies have been subsequently modified almost to the point of taking back what they said in the first place. I think it's fair to say, and I think most people experienced in the field would agree, that transforming the sustenance drinker into an occasional drinker is just blue smoke.

Any method of cutting down, as so many doctors recommend, probably is more difficult than chopping it off entirely. But to do that, the alcoholic needs help; self-control, willpower or determination won't work with alcoholism any better than with any other disease. Nor will drugs, despite the slaphappy dispensation of such medications as Valium. Emotional promises to quit are meaningless and eventually bring derisive snorts of laughter from families and friends. Inner strength is a beginning and a necessity, but it needs reinforcement through organized, experienced and sympathetic treatment.

Further, going cold turkey during the actual withdrawal—the detoxification—can be dangerous. It didn't bother me the dozen or so times I did it. For some, in some instances, it's a breeze. But many experts, including doctors, think it is at least as hazardous as withdrawal from hard drugs. It can produce ghastly DTs and, of course, convulsions. I was in one rehabilitation clinic where the plastic tongue depressors used to prevent strangulation during convulsions were placed in every room and along corridor walls. In all clinics they are kept close at hand, though not always so prominently. Delirium tremens can be frightening not only to the patient who has them but to bystanders and other patients. They can be extremely noisy and can monopolize the time of rugged male attendants until the patient is fully subdued. And they can do permanent damage. So withdrawal from alcoholism should not be a do-it-yourself project.

Less garish but maybe more deadly are the psychological aspects of withdrawal. Really gone alcoholics frequently talk of suicide. For the most part it is just talk, though it may scare the pants off the uninformed. Once in a great while, however, it is for real. An alcoholic, while still drinking, may become so depressed that suicide seems the only solution. The alcohol itself is a depressant. So are the tranquilizers and other sedatives used to ease alcoholic shock. The combination clearly can result in suicidal tendencies that must be understood and watched by people who are, through training, alert to the differences between despondent talk and despondent action.

Adding to the feeling of hopelessness during hangovers or withdrawals will be a drunk's sometimes subliminal realization that he is losing his primary escape. Alcohol is a splendid way to avoid reality. It is quick, easy to get, and carries no social stigma if used politely. It provides more than diversion; it obliterates reality, a condition that can be maintained twenty-four hours a day. This alone distinguishes it from most alternative common escapes. People may turn to work or excessive eating as a refuge. They may busy themselves with sports or hobbies or fraternal organizations or obsessive attention to their children. They may try music or bridge or incessant chatter or movies or perhaps the most important — sex. There are any number of other outlets. But, with possible exception of eating, they are only temporary diversions. You can't play golf twenty-four hours a day but you can stay more-or-less pleasantly polluted around the clock until you collapse. The person who uses alcohol as an escape will find it hard to replace. A good many ardent AA members use sobriety as a substitute, and that, while perhaps dull to outsiders, seems to work the best of all.

Misconceptions about alcoholism collectively constitute probably the greatest obstacle to its treatment. Of these misconceptions, the greatest is the almost unanimous opinion among the uninformed that a lush could cut down or quit entirely if he wasn't just a no-good bum to start with. In effect, he is notified that since he hasn't the guts to do it on his own, he's not worth bothering with and no one will do anything for him. The uninformed, by the way, in this instance include intelligent, educated people who pride themselves on being with-it; they are not confined to the bigots, the rabble-rousers and the tunnel-vision reformers.

The drunkard is afraid of the shame to which he thinks he will be subjected if he asks for help. He often won't tell his doctor or his clergyman. He shaves points, so to speak, when he tells anyone how much he drinks; almost invariably he will say he is a moderate drinker or an occasional drinker, almost never a heavy drinker. In part this is due, as has been noted before, to uneasiness at the prospect of being told to curtail or cease, but perhaps it is mostly a dread of social opprobium, the shame-on-you attitude that he feels is inevitable.

Actually, he should be proud that he is big enough, honest enough, and sensible enough to ask for help. He would be astonished at how many of his friends will reverse their attitudes and become proud of him. They are ashamed, not if he admits he needs help, but because he won't. If he does, scorn will turn to admiration; the alcoholic becomes proud of himself, and life is easier all the way around.

I cannot exactly be proud of myself, but I am pleased that, for whatever reason, I stood still after a fashion and let others pound some sense into me. I am pleased that I am sober, though I try my best not to be ostentatious or smug about it. When I discuss it, I try to be factual, not moral. As for being humiliated by or uncomfortable from my sobriety, I am afraid of the humiliation I would feel if I lost it.

A distinguishing characteristic of Alcoholics Anonymous is that nowhere is there a trace of embarrassment over the fact that participants needed and got help. The same is true for most alcoholism clinics. Only if you slip is there concern, and the concern is focused on getting the slipee back on sober, steady feet. The openness and mutual esteem so obvious at AA or at good rehabilitation centers are essential elements in any treatment and are perhaps most surprising to the person who has been buffeted his entire drinking career by the high winds of prejudice and midunderstanding.

So the alcoholic who could quit any time he wanted to must decide whether he wants to. It is easier on him and everyone else concerned if he decides he wants to before he hits rock-hard bottom. But that first step is a son of a bitch.

5

Okay, I'll Get Help

The bewildered drunk who capitulates and agrees he needs help is basically no better off until he decides what he is going to do about it. He has taken a heroic and essential step, but the next step becomes just as critical.

Four possible sources of help usually occur to those confronting the problem of alcoholism: a doctor, a psychiatrist, a minister, or Alcoholics Anonymous. In most cases, the first three are well-nigh useless. The fourth is magnificent if the patient will embrace it, but too many do not.

HELP FROM A DOCTOR

The average person will probably have great difficulty admitting the extent of his problem even to a physician. His version may range anywhere from, "I drink a little, but my wife thinks it's too much," to "I drink quite a bit, but I don't think I'm an alcoholic." Whatever the patient says, the doctor will make an independent determination, depending upon his own pattern of thinking. Seldom does he tell a patient bluntly that he has symptoms of all-out alcoholism that will be fatal if unrestrained. Customarily, the doctor will be more gentle.

My liver has on occasion been the size of a small watermelon, but never can I recall having been told pointblank to stop entirely the use of alcohol. When I asked the doctors later why they weren't rough with me they gave a variety of answers parallel to those given scores of others with whom I've talked. One common explanation is that they knew I would not quit, which was correct. In their view, the best they could hope for was a drastic reduction in booze, an imposition of self-control that they didn't seem to know was virtually impossible for a 100-percent-pure alcoholic. Equally common was the doctors' statement that tightly limited drinking was not necessarily bad and might even be good. Also correct, but under the circumstances also impossible.

Doctors have said they didn't want to drive us away to search for others who simply would not tell us what we did not want to hear. Additional reasons are offered, but I believe that among the more important is the natural inclination of many doctors to dish out bad news mildly, combined with a commendable feeling that they are not omniscient and should not be dogmatic. After all, most doctors are nice people and don't enjoy being the heavies. Nor are they so conceited as to believe they are infallible.

The doctors' uncertainties in handling alcoholics may be due, in large part, to their training. They have been taught, most of them, about the pathological results of alcoholism. They know it is a frequent cause of cirrhosis of the liver, ulcerated stomachs, pancreatitis, hypoglycemia, and other ailments. Yet they often do not lump the symptoms—the syndromes—into one basic disease. Perhaps the best way to make the point clear is through a story told me by one doctor who was for a time an instructor at a good medical school, which included a hospital. He would exhibit a patient who had all of the ailments listed above plus a few others associated with alcoholism. He would ask his student what was wrong and what treatments should be undertaken. They would propose direct treatment of the cirrhosis, the pancreatitis, the hypoglycemia; only once in a blue moon would a student, an intern or a resident suggest treatment for the underlying cause of all the difficulties—alcoholism.

This tendency to make two-plus-two equal one may help explain why death certificates seldom list alcoholism as the cause of death. Thousands a year should. Instead, the cause is put down as one of the symptoms of alcoholism, such as cirrhosis. While cirrhosis is not always the result of excessive drinking, when it is, it would seem reasonable to recognize alcoholism as the fatal disease. The error or ommission may be, in part, the result of social pressure. Until fairly recently—maybe forty years ago—it was considered gauche to refer to cancer—or even tuberculosis—as a cause of death. Alcoholism is still not considered a socially acceptable way to die.

The effects of alcohol on the body involve nothing shameful, nothing satanic. Alcohol is poison to the liver, for example, and the liver turns out an assortment of essential products, including factors that help in blood clotting. Without these factors, massive bleeding sometimes results from ulcers and from gastritis, an inflammation of the entire stomach lining. Both conditions can be the result of alcohol. The liver also breaks down the female sex hormone estrogen; when it cannot do the job properly men can develop large breasts and shrunken testicles. Then there is cirrhosis of the liver. The word cirrhosis comes from the Greek for a tawney-orange color, which presumably the liver will become when there is scarring of the liver cells. The liver has remarkable survival and recuperative powers, but it cannot function as the body's central factory—its Quartermaster Depot—if it is completely closed down by scar tissue. The development of cirrhosis seems to depend to some degree, at least, on the duration of drinking as well as on the quantity drunk.

Alcohol also can contribute to inflammation of the pancreas—pancreatitis. The pancreas produces insulin, which utilizes and burns up sugar in the body, and it produces digestive enzymes. Pancreatitis can be extremely painful and can ultimately result in diabetes—a high blood sugar. Alcohol also can figure in low blood sugar—hypoglycemia—which, like diabetes, can result in a distressing lack of energy, coma, and other serious symptoms.

Alcohol can do other deadly mischief, such as brain damage and a weakening of the heart's pumping muscles, which in turn can become congestive heart failure. Then there is cancer of the liver and throat, which studies indicate is encouraged by alcohol.

These are not farfetched examples of what booze can do. They are real, everyday happenings. The cause of these illnesses is not always alcohol, but alcohol is a frequent cause.

A person with alcohol-related difficulties will never get well until the alcohol is cut off; treating the effects of alcoholism will not reach the alcoholism. Many doctors do not seem to understand that alcoholism is a medical entity, for which treatment is not by direct means such as medication, diet, surgery, radiology or the myriad miracle measures now so skillfully employed by the profession. The treatment for alcoholism is abstract. It is not now tabulated in whatever doctors use for encyclopedias.

The fact that alcoholism is a specific disease but is not treatable as such makes it extremely difficult for doctors to handle. Treatment involves a great deal of time, concentration and energy, and a highly specialized knowledge.

A doctor could not spend twenty-eight days, ten hours a day, focusing on just one patient or one group of patients. He has other lives to worry about. The patient who gets half an hour of the doctor's time per visit is lucky. And unless the doctor has particular experience and training, he probably can't deal with the alcoholic's problem anyhow.

What the physician could do is learn to recognize alcoholism and its seriousness and know where to send a sufferer for further diagnosis and treatment, just as he knows were to send a heart patient or a cancer patient or multiple sclerosis patient. Many doctors now do suggest Alcoholics Anonymous but, as I have explained, that is not always enough.

Another basic obstacle to successful medical treatment of alcoholics is the fact that the doctors' ultimate weapon is fear and rarely is a drunk scared sober. If a doctor tells a patient he must quit drinking or he will die, he may frighten a lush into treatment—into AA or a clinic or other expedient—which is a big plus, but the treatment, not the doctor, does the actual work. Fear alone isn't effective, in part because alcohol can deaden, among other sensations, the feeling of fear itself. If an alcoholic is physically uncomfortable, the odds are he will try his own miracle remedy—a drink.

An even greater problem for the doctor may be the death wish. Many alcoholics often have true death wishes, as distinguished from the feelings of despair and depression that are part of conventional hangovers. The genuine death wish may be deeply buried; rarely will the alcoholic take quick and irreversible action such as jumping off a bridge. But he may, knowingly or otherwise, try to drink himself to death. Thus threats of an alcoholic demise may actually encourage the drinking. We have all known of people who have been told their liver difficulties will be fatal unless they end their boozing and a week later found them lapping it up at a disco bar.

HELP FROM PSYCHIATRISTS

I assume the awful dilemma of the death wish is a matter for psychiatric attention, but if the booze addict turns in that direction for general help with his alcoholism, he probably will be disappointed and discouraged. Many psychiatrists are forthright about it: they won't accept alcoholics as patients, even those who admit they need aid. The exclusion of alcoholic patients seems to be motivated in part by an awareness that the treatment of alcoholism is a specialized time-consuming field in which they may have had limited or no training. Treatment of a drunk involves a great measure of psychology, and is focused on one disease, yet it is diffused. And basically, the question of why a drunk is a drunk is most often unfathomable and unnecessary. Not all drinkers become addicts. Discovering the reason a person first tried alcohol doesn't explain why it consumed him.

To emphasize the point, professionals at alcoholic treatment centers often tell an apocryphal story of the desperate young drunkard who appealed to his psychiatrist to learn why he couldn't straighten out. After much costly time and effort, the psychiatrist finally determined with certainty that it all traced back to the fact that his mother had square nipples. The mother consented to corrective surgery to round off her nipples. The end of the parable, if that's what it is, is obvious. The operation made no measurable difference in the son's condition.

Psychiatrists also seem prone to confuse cause and

symptom. A psychiatrist will get a patient, for example, who is an alcoholic and who has severe mental problems, especially depression. The patient blames his alcoholism on his depression. The psychiatrist agrees; he treats the alcoholic for depression, not for alcoholism. This gives the alcoholic freedom to continue or intensify the drinking, which worsens the depression.

Those psychiatrists who don't feel qualified to handle an alcoholic or who don't want to bother, will often send a supplicant to one who is and does. Or they will try to steer the patient to Alcoholics Anonymous, and occasionally to a rehabilitation center. They also often will offer the standard consolation prize of a mess of tranquilizers. In my struggles, one psychiatrist regarded as a specialist in alcoholism, gave me two plastic bottles, each with one hundred fairly potent mood-elevating tranquilizers on a refillable prescription. Four years later I still have them, to exhibit not to take. I knew one sufferer who got, from one psychiatrist at one time, four hundred of the strongest downers.

A clinical or social psychologist can sometimes be more helpful than a psychiatrist. I wouldn't presume to know why, but from conversations with drunks who have tried both, one feature stood out: the psychologist gave them feedback. The patient did not just talk; when he lied or glossed over or misrepresented, he was punctured by the psychologist's analysis and fell back to reality with a thud. Also, there was less emphasis on why he started drinking and more on why he drank too much, plus harsh examinations of what it was doing to him and to those around him.

Professional family counselors also have pluses. They, too, tend to speak starkly and they—like psychologists—frequently recommend Alcoholics Anonymous or rehabilitation centers. The alcoholic who finally goes for help needs such exchanges. He needs to talk out his problem and he needs to be brought up short when he puts on an act. But he also may need a more intense atmosphere for a longer period of time, an atmosphere such as that provided to some degree by AA and to a greater degree by a rehab clinic.

HELP FROM THE MINISTRY

As for men of the cloth, many of the same points can be made about them as about doctors of medicine and psychiatry. One of the country's outstanding experts on alcoholism is a Catholic priest who is a "recovering" alcoholic. He has been recovering for perhaps a quarter of a century. His talks are delightful, informative and extremely effective. He learned, not as the result of his ministry but from bitter personal experience. He does not regard drinking as merely a weakness, a sin, or a deviation. His fight to overcome it unquestionably was reinforced by his sublime faith in the Almighty. But he nonetheless knows alcoholism as a disease and he is devoted to relieving the suffering it brings.

Most clerics who have not been through the anguish of alcoholism are convinced it can be conquered by determination and inner strength, with God's help. I thought of that often, as I took note of the number of ministers of all faiths among my colleagues at various drunk tanks—rehabilitation centers. God will help the believer, but He too needs help. If a drunk in search of aid is lucky enough to find a minister who has knowledge of, and been exposed to, alcoholics, he may benefit a great deal. But the record indicates that faith alone rarely is enough. This seems to be generally true whether the minister uses quiet logic or fire-and-brimstone fundamentalism. Once again, fear infrequently brings sobriety, though it be fear of the hereafter and a heavenly blacklist.

Alcoholism would seem beyond the ken of many, probably most, doctors of medicine, doctors of psychiatry and doctors of divinity. There are exceptions, of course, as there are to most generalizations about alcoholics. But the treatment of alcoholics requires special knowledge, special wisdom and special dedication that more often comes from personal experience than from books or lectures.

ALCOHOLICS ANONYMOUS

Religious faith is an integral part of the teachings of Alcoholics Anonymous although commendable efforts are made to camouflage the fact sufficiently to allow non-believers to participate. AA relies on what it calls a Higher Power for support, and its literature labels the Higher Power "God." But the newcomer is assured that his Higher Power can be absolutely anything—a tree, a wheelbarrow, a river, an empty paint can. Literally. To many AA enthusiasts—a group that includes agnostics and atheists and pagans—the symbolism is very real. The theory, I assume, is that the confused, harassed drunk must fix on something for spiritual reinforcement.

Nonetheless, the religious aspects of Alcoholics Anonymous repel many who need its help. Or, to put it more honestly, they give a recalcitrant drunk an excuse for not embracing AA, an excuse for avoiding any interruption in his drinking. More times than my computer could count, I have heard variations of the expression, "I can't put up with all that religious crap," from people who had made feeble efforts to get with AA. I have argued endlessly that the miserable drunk, if he really wanted help, could get a great deal from AA without compromising his non-religious attitude. I even go so far as to disclose that I chose for my own "higher power" the need to make amends to my dead wife. But even such personal and private confessions seldom make a dent.

The determined drunk can think up a variety of other reasons for rejecting AA. I shall not go into minute detail on what goes on at a typical AA meeting, partly because there is no such thing and partly because I interpret the word "anonymous" strictly. Also, details might provide the evader with additional excuses for not giving AA an honest try. And an explicit dissertation on how it functions might somehow diminish its mysterious power to do good.

Vast numbers of people know how AA works, but I have found no consensus of why it works. The mechanics are simple. It is not an organization; "fellowship" is the preferred description and is more apt. There is no centralized headquarters authority; each group has its own routines, sets its own rules and determines its own schedules. Technically, no one is a member; you attend or not as you please. No last names are used, there are no membership lists, and no dues. At most meetings a collection is taken and voluntary contributions of no fixed amounts constitute the major financing.

Generally, meetings are of two types—open and closed. At open meetings, which anyone can attend, recovering alcoholics make speeches, telling their own stories. Some are funny, as reminiscences; some are tragic, or poignant, or even revolting. Above all, they are frank and honest. They cover a tremendous variety of human behavior; they range from the man who shut himself in a rented room for nine months, with his misguided female friend bringing him what little food he ate and the enormous amounts of booze he drank, to the relatively prosperous gentleman who headed for the nearest airport when he was bombed and took off for Geneva, Hong Kong, Aukland, or the farthest point he could reach on available flights.

Closed meetings, on the other hand, are theoretically limited to admitted alcoholics. They consist largely of group discussions of personal problems related to alcohol and of the intricacies and nuances of AA teachings particularly as embodied in the justly famous Twelve Steps to Sobriety. These, too, cover a wide range and take in every conceivable psychological and physical difficulty a drunk can experience.

A meeting rarely lasts more than an hour. "Members" go as frequently as they feel the need. I have known some to make two meetings a day, seven days a week. In large cities there is a meeting somewhere at almost any hour of the day or night. If no meeting is available and a member feels he is cracking, he is free to telephone any other member, or a stipulated central location, and talk out his crisis. So anxious are members of the organization to help that calls at four in the morning are commonplace and usually taken cheerfully and seriously.

The reasons a frightened alcoholic would resist AA include skepticism about the anonymity, especially in small towns where gossip is the main recreation. Also, to one who has consistently denied his drinking problem, the frankness can be shocking—beginning one's remarks with, "I am an alcoholic," then stripping off all the protective coverings that have been for years so carefully built up, almost bragging in front of others about how drunk one has been. But once an alcoholic participates actively, or even if he listens long enough, he gets relief through the very circumstances about which he was most dubious.

The primary requirement for getting the most out of AA is an intense desire for help, a desire without reservations of any kind. Many wise veterans of the movement think an alcoholic can be helped only after he has hit absolute bottom, that he must be a total disaster, must be in a well-nigh worthless condition before his desire to quit will make him receptive. More optimistic experts think it's worth trying to assist an alcoholic before he reaches the stage of complete disintegration and degradation. Whichever philosophy is operating, AA exposure will be most effective if the alcoholic can be persuaded to attend meetings regularly, though he may consider them dull and useless when he starts. Also, he should shop around, go to meetings of a number of different groups, until he finds one or several that best suit him. But it can take time. One friend whom I enticed into trying AA dutifully went three nights a week to a number of different groups for six months, usually protected by a couple of pre-meeting drinks, then suddenly got the idea and hasn't had even one dollop since. Unfortunately, some AA groups seem cold and standoffish to the newcomer, particularly in smaller towns or in strictly neighborhood gatherings. In some larger meetings, cliques of old-timers almost inevitably develop and the freshman, however eager, has trouble penetrating.

To help ease entry, each new man or woman can easily get a sponsor, often through a friend who is already active in the fellowship or by simply calling the Alcoholics Anonymous number in the telephone book. The sponsor, for the best results, should know people in different groups, take his charge to meetings, get him started by explaining the procedures and introducing him to other veterans, who will in turn introduce him to others. In other words, the sponsor should make the newcomer feel comfortable and welcome. That's what fellowship should mean. I was lucky enough to get an excellent sponsor, but it doesn't always work, particularly with those who don't really want it to.

Objections to AA seem perfectly valid to the person in question, but they can be met. The biggest drawback to AA lies not with those who would give help, but with those who need help. The organization—the fellowship—prides itself on never wittingly rejecting anyone. But the fellowship itself is rejected by a high percentage of those who need it most.

I now rarely go to AA meetings, but I certainly do not reject them. The rehabilitation centers softened me up so thoroughly that when I got out I welcomed the fellowship at which I once sneered. I went four nights a week for approximately a year while it slowly sank in that alcohol was no longer a factor of any kind in any part of my life, so I gradually cut down. I consider myself an extraordinarily fortunate person, since I no longer have any temptation to fend off. The rehabilitation clinics obviously did a magnificent job of changing my direction, and AA did a magnificent job of maintenance and strengthening. And if I ever feel even the slightest twinge of craving I will be back at AA and probably get a speeding ticket on the way.

6

Rehabilitation Centers

When someone goes into a rehabilitation clinic, he faces a complete overhaul. Not just a valve job or new rings but The Works. The paint and trim the patient will have to do himself, but they come easy once the machinery is operating smoothly and pride of ownership is restored.

Two recovering alcoholics told me before my first go-round with treatment that whether I quit drinking or not, I would never be the same again. They were right. I know I became a better person, and although my drinking became much worse after my wife died, I never forgot the lessons I had learned, which made it easier to get back on the tracks later. I am convinced the same is true of many others who are derailed after treatment.

I shall not attempt to probe deeply the methods of treatment. In the first place, I am not qualified; also, divulging too many details might damage the chances of other patients. But I believe I can lay out the characteristics of what might be considered a typical rehabilitation center and outline some of the approaches to give a fair picture of what the alcoholic might expect. Many centers, of course, don't fit the pattern at all. A few can be considered totally unorthodox, which does not mean they won't work.

WHAT ARE THESE PLACES???

In-patient rehabilitation centers can be sumptuous or stark, rural or urban, comfortable and cozy or the contrary. Some have recreational facilities—even golf, tennis and hot tubs; others are all work. Some allow limited supervised frivolity such as group singing, square dancing, and similar supposed tension-relievers. Some allow visitors only on weekends; others have quarters where families can stay to help patients sweat it out and to get instructions in how to handle live-in alcoholics. Some allow phone calls; others try to prevent them. Each operates somewhat differently and some are more effective with certain types of people than with others.

The "typical" rehabilitation center will have a course of treatment running about twenty-eight days, not including five to eight days at the start of detoxification, if required. The course usually will cost from about $2,500 up, way up, plus a minimum of close to $1,000 for detoxification. The country club types generally are more expensive, but price does not accurately indicate quality. One I consider among the best is also among the cheapest. The fancy places are not always rated highly by the tougher professional therapists, nor by the hardened rehabilitation veterans who may have been in and out of clinics for years. One woman confided to me that she could remember being in twenty-three such institutions, and admitted she probably had forgotten several. She felt strongly that the tougher they were and the fewer distractions they permitted, the more they benefitted her. But with her record, it's hard to say what "benefitted" means.

The typical center, if there is such a thing, is deliberately tough to impress upon the patient how serious the problem is. It has tight discipline, rigid routines, lectures and group therapy, an occasional short movie, early rising, light assigned chores, and rarely any drugs—not even aspirin—after detoxification.

This last restriction seemed silly to me, until I found out about what some of us in the *milieu* call "garbage heads." Garbage heads are compulsive pill-takers and in alcoholic clinics are found among the cross-addicted. They have taken uppers and downers and in-betweeners at every opportunity for so long that it has become a hand-habit. If they see a bottle of pills, no matter what they are, they will swallow them, apparently on the theory that any pills are better than no pills. Breaking the garbage head's habit is important, and one way is to have no pills around. In one long turbulent evening, an unfortunate man I knew took approximately forty medium size Valium, three to five at a time, washed down with vodka. Nobody knew the exact pill count, but the man lived, after a short sojourn in the hospital.

The proper starting point for describing the workings of a rehabilitation facility is at the front door. A reservation has been made. The patient may be floundering drunk; some establishments that do their own detoxifying encourage them to be. If a supplicant has been drinking during the days preceding admittance, he will need detoxification anyhow, and if he is in his customary flabby state, he will be that much easier to handle. At one place, as I watched, a car drove up with a man and woman in front, and a 72-year-old sack of jelly sprawled in the back. Attendants pulled mightily on the old man, seemed about to rip him apart, but could not get him out until someone discovered his seat belt was fastened.

Anyhow, the patient stays in a semi-stupor while the

alcohol is eliminated from his system. If a patient doesn't need detoxification, he is put directly in the main group.

Then starts the grind. He is awakened early, is supposed to make his own bed in time for a 6:30 or 7 A.M. breakfast, which in itself is a shock to a large number of the disorganized, disoriented clients. Many have extreme difficulty getting to sleep in the first place, what with the various upheavals in their lives, plus the fact that if they have a roommate, his snoring can be relied upon to register between six and eight on the Richter Scale.

After breakfast comes the first lecture or therapy session, and then another. After lunch, a recess can be devoted to such fascinating pursuits as socializing, walking, reading, or napping. An afternoon meeting can come either before or after the recess, and at long last, dinner. After dinner, maybe another social period, and another meeting, sometimes a regular AA meeting. Finally, it's to bed—sometimes under curfew, sometimes not.

The next day is the same. All the days are the same except for weekends, when church attendance is permitted and visitors are allowed. Checks are made during the week to make sure nobody is skipping classes.

A patient won't be allowed off the immediate premises for the first few days; then he is allowed out only when accompanied by at least one other person, generally another patient. This is less to prevent escape than to minimize the chances of a patient being diverted from the job at hand before he has a chance to synchronize with the routine—before he is innoculated, so to speak. If he has a car, in a non-urban environment, he usually has to surrender the keys; with wheels, he can almost always find a saloon. He is allowed to have money at most places, for all the good it will do him.

It is clear why the majority of inmates are miserably unhappy the first couple of weeks. They don't want to be there in the first place. A tremendous percentage still cannot face the prospect of a future without firewater. They don't know their classmates. They loath the regimentation and what they consider the harshness and lack of respect with which they are handled. They resent the isolation, being cut off from their families and friends and their neighborhood bars and parties. They think they are in a prison, wasting a month of their lives when they might be having fun. And they don't think the treatment will do a particle of good.

Some will try any device to get out. Customarily, a good number will have every legal right, as I did, simply to walk away, but few will try it and fewer will succeed for reasons I will go into later.

Plots to get sprung frequently include friendly or phoney doctors as accomplices. A friendly doctor, perhaps an old drinking buddy of the patient, is persuaded to telephone the clinic, or even come in person, to suggest or demand his pal be released because of a heart condition or hypertension or some other disorder he contends requires constant attention and an intimate knowledge of the patient's medical history. A phoney doctor—again he can be an old drinking buddy—telephones, but rarely will make a personal appearance to press his case. Or the doctor or "doctor" will tell the center's management that the patient's child or sister or mother or somebody is critically sick and requires the patient's services and support. As a matter of course, the center will check with the patient's nearest of kin. In spite of such precautions, a colleague at one clinic, after faking a couple of minor heart attacks, had his doctor theoretically take him to a regular hospital for extensive tests. That's the last the clinic saw of him. The clinic listed him on their records as "AWOL," which shows how the supervisors feel about their institutions.

The pressures that keep patients from skulking out

are about equal to those encountered by a deep-diving submarine. Some of the pressures are direct: a patient is taking treatment under court order and the alternative is a stiff prison term; he is following the mandate of a federal, state or local government agency and the alternative is formal court action; he is under an ultimatum for his employer to change his habits or change jobs.

Families can exert tremendous force, not only psychological but financial. The psychological is quite apparent: threats to force the alcoholic out of the family and, in effect, into the gutter. Also, in those areas where it is possible, threats of having him committed to a state institution as incompetent. In some states it's easy.

These overlap some of the financial forces, such as the possibility of divorce proceedings on charges that could deprive him of his home and most of his possessions. Father and mother can declare the probability of total estrangement and disinheritance. Parents can have even greater power, at least in theory, over the younger drinkers, the teen-age alcoholics.

Other factors in keeping the patient docile come from within the patient himself. Somewhere deep inside is a glimmer of hope that the treatment will work and a feeling of chagrin at the prospect that he might not be able to go through such a relatively gentle purgatory. He tends to develop a sense of pride in taking his beatings—and curiosity about what's coming next in the planned therapy.

But by far the most effective influence is peer pressure. It is, literally, on all sides. Whether the patients are put together in one group, or divided into a number of separate groups as in the larger establishments, a major part of the discipline is left to the groups themselves. If a patient tries or decides to leave, the problem is brought up for discussion at a group meeting, sometimes on an emergency basis. The other group members almost invariably will be unanimous in ganging up on the dissident trying every known form of persuasion. The decisive reason probably is the fact that they truly care. They don't want the patient to give up; they know it is likely to be his last chance and they know the alternatives. They may flunk out themselves, some of them, but they cannot bear the thought of some other unfortunate surrendering.

Also, being in the majority with the good guys gives them a feeling of self-righteousness. For once in their lives, they are doing the right thing.

And they think it will improve their standings with the therapists whose approval they crave, the way children crave the approval of teachers.

When a patient tries to sneak away, the situation can turn into a soap-opera drama. One of "my" centers was set in a patch of pastureland, remote from any neighbors except a tiny village and a bar, which incidentally would not serve a customer if the proprietor suspected he was a patient at the drunk farm. About 11 o'clock one warm, pleasant fall evening, we got word that one of the patients had taken off. He was a tough coal miner who played and sang country music that was entrancing, at least to us, and he was very well liked. Six or seven of us, without waiting for authorization, immediately went after him and caught him down the road. He was determined and bellicose; he had been in the institution only five days. We surrounded him and argued until we were panting. Finally he made two fearsome fists and told us to get the hell out of his way or he would blast through. The rescuers promptly put together a collection of less formidable fists and said they would beat him to a pulp if they had to, but they were not letting him go.

He returned, and about a week later approached each of us, not to criticize or apologize, but to thank us. He finished the course and the last I heard was sailing serenely through a boozeless life.

He was a fine example of alcoholic thinking: he had nowhere to go; the nearest big town was fifteen or twenty miles away. He had no money, except small change; he was beyond the reach of taxis or any other form of transportation and the surrounding country roads were deserted at that time of night. Such physical difficulties can be a formidable deterrent. Even in urban areas, the centers' doors are usually locked or under surveillance by alert attendants. And if a patient does manage to get out without permission, he also is likely to be pursued by a band of inmate-vigilantes.

An even more drastic escape method is a deliberate effort to get thrown out. It takes some doing, since the behavior of most patients right after detoxification is unpredictable, to put it conservatively. Very seldom is there violence, but there is a variety of other unusual conduct, such as refusing to talk, attending but refusing to participate in therapy sessions, or refusing to eat. To be expelled usually requires pretty dramatic action.

An attractive young woman at one center managed to get the heave within three days by smuggling in a quantity of amphetamines. High as a satellite, she sat all night in the lounge telling filthy stories, describing her own sexual exploits in explicit fashion, and propositioning the eager men and women who would stay up to listen to her coarse and unimaginative language. Still on her garrulous high, she was shipped back to the welfare and police sources who sent her to the center in the first place. I scarcely knew her, but she had confided to me when she first arrived what she intended to do, and it worked.

A patient also can be ejected if it becomes apparent he is getting nothing out of the course, and does not want to. A highly successful businessman came into one center under duress; his boss had told him it was either-or—either sobriety or unemployment. The businessman vehemently denied he drank and considered the whole thing a joke. After several warnings that he was not sufficiently involved in the program, he decided to go through the motions and finish the course with honors. He threw himself into therapy sessions, figured out all the right answers to anything he was asked, did everything he thought he was supposed to do. But it was obvious he was faking; nothing had sunk in. On the 27th day, supposedly his next-to-last day, he was abruptly expelled, an action often called "shock therapy." If the expulsion would not jolt him into sobriety, nothing would. He was extremely unhappy and angry. He was picked up by a limousine and on his way back to New York stopped at the very first cocktail bar. Through mutual acquaintances I learned he had no job when he got home, nor did he have his wife and two children or legal title to his Westchester house. He even was barred from his beloved country club.

Surprisingly, a great many patients are, in a way, reluctant to leave the centers as departure gets near. It isn't necessarily that they love the place; they are afraid. By the third week or so, they are all charged up with the idea of getting off alcohol. They want sobriety more than anything else in the world. They love the joys that go with sobriety and they remember the woes that came from drinking. But they are not sure it will last.

They have, for a month, been sheltered and reinforced. They have not been exposed to the lure of alcohol nor to the vexations they have so long used as excuses for drinking. And they are uncertain about how they will react when removed from this comfortable, protected nest. Almost every "graduate" has some of these misgivings, but with a few it is a genuine dread.

This is one reason practically every good rehabilitation spot, as its last word to the parting patients, urges attendance at Alcoholics Anonymous meetings. AA can lead a graduate through the valley of temptation.

So, for one reason or another, almost all patients stick it out and perversely many begin to enjoy the experience after a couple of weeks. They probably still want to get out but they want to finish what they started. They begin to appreciate the insights they are getting, as well as the advantages of sobriety and the social distinction it gives them. They begin to understand the agonies they have gone through, the distress they have brought to others, and the money they wasted getting and staying drunk.

They leave with regret what they conceive to be deep and significant friendships they have made at the center and the constant availability of confidantes with whom they can discuss their emotions and travails.

Just shows you cannot outguess an alcoholic.

THE COMPLETE OVERHAUL

Some clinics deliberately start out by cutting a patient down to size—by humiliating him in little ways, by degrading him, by stripping away whatever ego he may have left. Various papers written on the subject would indicate that the objective is to make the alcoholic an almost helpless psychological pulp, sufficiently limp to accept any measure that will restore his self-confidence. But the puzzling part is that a good many patients, perhaps most, are already in that shape when they come into the center, so why use such tactics on them?

Perhaps—probably—it is useful to strip away any bit of protective facade that may be left in order to achieve the No. 1 goal of convincing the stubborn alcoholic that he is an alcoholic. But numerous other devices also are used—a combination of approaches that for thoroughness would do credit to the planning for the Normandy invasion.

In therapy groups, the patient will be coaxed and coerced into talking about himself and why and how he wound up where he is. He will be questioned sharply by his colleagues, particularly about how he could fail to realize he is an alcoholic in view of what he has told them. He may be prodded into making an inventory of himself, along the lines of the famous Fourth Step of Alcoholics Anonymous. Efforts will be made to make him see himself objectively, as others see him.

His inventory should include the good qualities as well as the bad. It helps convince him that he is worth saving—that he's not all bad; it also usually makes him see that most of his bad qualities, his so-called "character defects," are most evident when, and are generally related to, drinking. Many patients have more difficulty enumerating their good qualities than their bad; the good is buried under the garbage of the bad.

The inventory should be continuous, not just a project of the moment. It should undergo periodic updating long after the patient leaves the center. Some patients, even when not told to, write out their inventories so they can refer to them during periods of introspection, and thus judge for themselves whether they are continuing to improve or whether they have drifted backward. The inventories should be as complete and as cruelly honest as the subjects can make them. They should dredge up every evil (or good) they have ever done by design and habit. If they are totally frank with their inventories and if they take them seriously, the alcoholics' views and opinions of themselves will be drastically changed.

Instead of, or along with, the inventories, each patient can be required to prepare an autobiographical description of his drinking career: when it started and how it progressed. It includes, at least in outline, the hideous and the merely regrettable things he did. This story, too, should be revised as the patient remembers things he had forgotten. Later, it can be a jim-dandy reminder what a fool he was—any time he feels tempted to return to booze. He should never forget his actions, but by the same token he should not dwell on them, should not become morbidly absorbed with them, corroded by guilt and shame. He should remind himself of them only when it is strategically important in his efforts not to repeat them. He was sick at the time and he doesn't want to be sick again.

The therapy sessions, although obviously directed toward alcoholism, generally resemble group therapy anywhere else. Patients to be focused on at particular sessions are selected pretty much at random and often by accident. The other patients will ask amazingly penetrating and intimate questions about the target's most private actions and thoughts. If such questions were asked in a different environment they might well provoke fights. But somehow, the victim of the inquisition will answer quietly, usually trying to be honest and sometimes making it. Generally, these groups do not reach for the screaming, tortured, fist-throwing, primal-scream stages that so often seem to be the ultimate goal of some therapy sessions.

Ideally, they will be guided by a therapist who actually will participate as little as possible. Theoretically, one patient learns by digging into the other patient's psyche, exposing things wrong that the other patient would not admit or did not know were there. And the patient himself presumably profits even more from having to confront his own character defects.

Rarely can a patient mislead an entire group; more rarely can he trick a really good therapist. A good therapist has been through the works himself and knows all the angles, or he has learned them from others and from books. All but one of the therapists I had was a recovering alcoholic, and most of them had branched out into drugs during their turbulent days. My favorite, the one who did me the most good, was from what is customarily referred to as a "fine family," had an excellent educational background and considerable economic and social advantages. But she had wound up an outstanding tramp among tramps. She not only was a far-out alcoholic, she had used every known drug, including heroin mainlined and in quantity. She had also mainlined speed for ungodly periods. She had participated in every conceivable form of debauchery and had resorted to prostitution to pay her drug bills. Somehow she straightened out and was, when I knew her, one of the finest people in every respect I ever met.

Another therapist was a young man who did not drink nor was he on drugs of any kind. But he was devoted to his task of helping people like me and his book learning had made him good at his work. After months of listening to the likes of me, he decided he had to try some of this alcohol himself—to round out his education. Within a year, he was hooked, had to be sent to another clinic to take the treatments he had been giving. He is now back at his old job and has become, I am told, one of the best.

The good therapist's devotion to the cause is almost frightening. I have known only a couple who were cavalier toward their patients. One was, in my opinion, a smartass who might have been effective if he had known twice as much as he thought he did. The other considered himself, by his own appraisal, intellectually objective; he would give the patients the benefit of his wisdom, what they did with it was their own responsibility.

But most therapists are immersed in their work. Each ministers to hundreds of derelicts and would-be derelicts every year, yet becomes totally involved with almost every patient. I have seen hard-bitten old-timers actually cry when one of their charges blew it. It wasn't that the therapist blamed himself, though that may have been a factor. It was more that he simply could not accept the idea that someone was condemning himself to the agony that the therapist himself had been through.

As a result, the job is exhausting. An official of one state program told me he estimated his useful career in his chosen line at no more than five to seven years. I was subsequently told that, after seven years, he reluctantly switched positions. He said he was burned out.

In some centers, the therapists themselves give lectures, usually recitations of their own experiences, very much like the talks given in open AA meetings except often more detailed and more horrible. The speeches tend to establish a tie between teacher and pupil, to show how low an alcoholic can sink and still be brought to the surface and live a useful life. Also, they serve as warnings that the therapists cannot be fooled, that they know and have tried every trick a drunk can conjure up.

Other lectures, at a good center, can cover every phase of alcoholism, from the medical to the purely emotional. The medical dissertations are less gory than the old-fashioned harangues about Demon Rum. They tend to be low-key, factual, and believable. Those dealing with the emotional side emphasize the insatiable, overwhelming nature of an addiction to alcohol, with the damage it can do the alcoholic in his relations with others and with himself.

The premise that an alcoholic must stop drinking for his own sake is heavily stressed. He shouldn't quit for the benefit of his wife or children or parents or girlfriend. He should put his own welfare first. Benefits will flow automatically to the others involved.

By building up and understanding himself, an alcoholic gradually restores his self-esteem and that, in turn, increases his will to leave the booze alone. If he uses someone else as a primary reason, he is likely to fall flat on his donkey. A wife may decide the fire is out and cannot be re-lit; whether he is drunk or sober, she does not want him as an active husband. Children may follow the same general route—and children do grow up and often fade out of the life of the most solicitous parent. My own was a case in point. I quit primarily for my wife's sake and she died.

The "me-first" approach is difficult for many people. Their self-confidence and self-regard may be so low that they feel they are not worth fiddling with. Age also can be a factor; an older person may well figure that, since he has only a few years to go, why put up with the tribulations of quitting. I had both these mental handicaps. But as for age—at the two treatment centers that I can best remember, there were a total of half-a-dozen men and women in their seventies and only one flopped out.

Here, as everywhere else in the alcoholic scene, there are exceptions. One wealthy and very prominent young stud wanted to quit for two reasons the professionals considered irrelevant. One, his drinking had ruined his social standing; his elegant Blue Book friends no longer found him acceptable. Two, the impotence brought on by excessive drinking had wiped out his Stud Book rating; his jet set friends no longer found him enjoyable. But he himself considered these two factors so important that he made it and the last I heard was slowly inching his way back, so to speak.

One of the serious hazards during treatment is having the patient include himself out—or count himself out, depending on what dialect you are speaking. At any rehabilitation center, and at AA too, for that matter, you will hear stories of alcoholic misbehavior that will make your teeth curl. The listener will realize that others have pulled things that he never would think of. He never chased his wife with an axe, never tried to rape his daughter, never walked naked into a formal dinner attended by the President of the United States, never threw his baby son out of a third-floor window, never stabbed to death his neighbor's yapping dog, never shot a cop, never . . . and on and on. He will conclude, from the evidence, that since he did not do these things, he is not an alcoholic. He chooses to ignore the evidence on the other side and contents himself by saying, in effect, I never did anything that bad.

This type patient is looking for some such rationalization to start with, and his alcoholic thinking persuades him he has found it. The idea can become so deeply entrenched that it is extremely difficult to tear out.

Another danger lies in what is often called "over-intellectualizing" the drinking problem. When a patient goes into a long far-fetched analysis of his addiction, he is considered to be over-intellectualizing. Also, he probably has read too many paperbacks on psychology.

I have heard alcoholism blamed on everything from a sensitivity to weather changes, to the color of the living room walls, to intricate job problems. It is all a waste of time. Alcoholism is a disease and if the victim had not used one excuse, he would have used another. Almost never is a person forced to take his first drink but from then on, it is Russian roulette.

These hazards are handled in group meetings and by lectures and films. But one of the most effective methods develops quite naturally during socializing at the centers. The conversations during informal social periods deal to a surprising extent with alcoholism. After even a few days in an acceptable clinic, alcoholism so pervades the atmosphere, and the other outside interests of the individual patients so vary, that alcoholism is the only subject they have in common.

Most patients find themselves trying to see something in other patients' stories with which they can identify. They also are interested, to a degree, in how the other person is handling the problem. From these dialogs can come a far greater appreciation of how low an alcoholic has sunk and how pleasant it would be to avoid in the future the suffering, the guilt, and the shame of continuing. They also can dramatize for the alcoholic the dangers and futility of drinking, and the truth of the temperance adage that there is no problem a drink won't make worse. Almost never does the talk involve sermonizing; patients who preach are ostracized.

The social periods often have another large plus going for them; they will show the beat-up alcoholic that others really do care, really are concerned about his welfare. As a matter of fact, any worthwhile alcoholic program, including AA, is built on the foundation of caring. Everybody the alcoholic meets—from the gardener to the therapist to the director—is genuinely concerned about his welfare.

Before he realizes this simple fact, the patient will have his ups-and-downs. He will feel he is being mauled; he will dread the day he comes up for group-therapy dissection; he worries about what his peers think of him, and whether he will "pass" the course and graduate, or whether he will flunk out. He wants to impress his therapist with his sincerity but he dares not fake it. And most of all, if the treatment is working, he wants to make it, wants to keep up the good work. Yet he may dream, in spite of himself, of having a drink—just one or maybe two—when he gets out.

This is where Alcoholics Anonymous comes in. As I have said, many—perhaps most—rehabilitation centers are based on AA teachings. One of the primary objectives is to soften up the patients to accept AA. A departing patient is urged—begged—to go to AA meetings every day for months, for support. Seven days a week for six months is a common recommendation. It works, in an amazing number of cases.

Nobody really knows how to measure statistically the success of any rehabilitation program. Some make claims—60 percent, 70 percent, 80 percent of their patients quit drinking—but none can be substantiated. One thing is certain: any good program is worth trying. The odds are in the drunk's favor, and he has nothing to lose.

7

High Noon

Getting a pig-headed alcoholic into intensive treatment can make jibbering wrecks of those attempting to help. It is like trying to find a blown fuse in the dark, or driving the freeway in a midnight fog. You don't know where you are or where you're going, you don't know what you are doing, and you don't know how it is going to end.

An obdurate alcoholic is one who, for one reason or another, has not benefitted from conventional treatment, including Alcoholics Anonymous. Usually, he has turned down or turned off assistance. And he flatly rejects rehabilitation.

Sometimes the process of reversing his decision can be fairly simple. The alcoholic may cave in if he or she is worked over for awhile; an appreciable number are susceptible to quiet one-on-one or two-on-one persuasion. But this presupposes an alcoholic whose thought processes are still somewhat orderly, and that is uncommon.

Sometimes, without warning, a drunk will switch his position and decide to accept help after all; more often than not, this docility can be traced to an unexpected psychological jolt such as a bad car accident or loss of a job. One moderately exalted federal official had been pounded verbally for an extended time by friends, relatives, and rescue workers from Alcoholics Anonymous with no results whatever. One day he passed out in his office while his boss was present. That evening I took my first crack at him, and two days later he was in a rehabilitation center—not because of me, but because of his own faux pas. He even helped pack his own bag, but so misty was his mind that he insisted on taking along six large boxes of those old-fashioned, foot-long fireplace matches, even though it was summer, the place he was going had no fireplace, and he did not smoke.

There are other circumstances under which commitment for treatment can be relatively easy. The alcoholic can be committed by the courts; in some areas, that is simple. Or if he has become an uncomprehending gelatinous blob, he can just be spooned into a car and taken to a treatment center. This happened to me, and I have done it to others. I call it "kidnapping," but I have never investigated the legal nuances of abducting an inanimate object that happens to have a faint pulse.

Otherwise, getting an uncooperative alcoholic into a proper institution involves not only finesse, but work—planning, preparation, perseverance—all aimed at a show-down confrontation that is rarely pleasant. During a confrontation the drunk is told he must get the works or the jig is up. It is the main event. It's the last play of the game, the 35-foot putt on the sudden-death playoff, the stretch run in the Derby.

In organizing for a confrontation, first must come a determination—and an inflexible decision—that the drunk urgently needs the ultimate treatment. His resistance, artifices, and excuses must not be allowed to shift attention from the basic goal. From that point on, every action must be tailored to the alcoholic; his emotional, physical, and mental makeup must be carefully considered.

Entirely different tactics may be required for the professional man, the "man in the street," the intellectual, the athletic type, or the home-loving type. Only those trying to help can figure out the proper approach. One condition, however, is assumed for each target: a rehabilitation program of some sort is the only chance left.

WEEDING AND PICKING

Selecting a rehabilitation center is the next item. The process can be tough and tiresome. The best way to start is by discussing the problem with relatives and friends, overcoming any embarrassment about bringing it into the open. You can bet your bottom kruggerand that you will not have to go far before turning up names of rehabilitation centers in your general area; you will get much more sympathetic attention than you expect.

If necessary, try the telephone book and the Yellow Pages. If you and the alcoholic are in a rural spot, try telephone books for the entire area and for the nearest larger cities. Your state, county, or town most likely has an agency dealing with alcoholism and in some cases can be a rewarding source of information:

—If you have, or hear of, a doctor or psychiatrist or clergyman who specializes in alcoholism, he can be useful.

—Perhaps the most fruitful sources are the local affiliates of the National Council on Alcoholism; providing such information is one of the Council's most important functions. (See Appendix I)

—Try psychological social workers or family counselors, whether private or governmental; you frequently hit jackpot.

—Activists in Alcoholics Anonymous sometimes are good sources; their one handicap can be that they honestly cannot understand why anyone needs more than the fellowship and consequently do not know about or do not care about rehabilitation centers.

—Almost any establishment with "alcohol" or drug treatment in its name is worth checking.

Weed out the places you consider least desirable because of location or other pertinent features.

Look and look and look—if you have to—until you find what you think is required. It might take weeks. On the other hand, you might get lucky and turn up exactly what you want the first crack out of the box. In my case, the first three friends my family sought out mentioned the same spot, which turned out to be customized for me and not exorbitantly priced.

Ask Questions

Start checking those places left on your list, beginning, of course, with those most highly recommended and most convenient. If feasible, visit them, see what they look like, ask questions.

Ask whether the center does its own detoxification and how. If not, a saturated patient might first have to go to a hospital. Finding a separate facility or hospital for detoxification could involve more time and more money, plus the inconvenience of tugging a recalcitrant blob from point to point. One of the advantages of an alcoholism care center that is attached to a hospital is the easy access to detoxification (and other) medical facilities.

Detoxification methods vary. The objective in every case is to get all alcohol out of the system without triggering delirium tremens, convulsions, or other developments that can be extremely dangerous. The most-used detoxification therapy seems to be centered around generous doses of tranquilizers, along with vitamins and quantities of fluids, given intravenously if necessary.

Another detoxification method includes the use of drugs, along with graduated ministrations of alcohol, beginning with a few ounces a day and dwindling to none as the detox progresses. This procedure may make detoxification more agreeable for the patient and probably doesn't do any harm, but there is controversy about whether it contributes anything not supplied by tranquilizers. In either case, the patient should be off all tranquilizers and alcohol when the detoxification process is completed.

Medical Supervision

Another area to be explored is that of medical facilities. Recovering alcoholics should be carefully watched for complications and for signs of illness that could have been camouflaged by alcoholic intake. Many experts on alcoholism prefer centers attached to general hospitals because extensive medical help is always close. Some rehabilitation centers have their own small hospitals and fulltime staff doctors. But these facts mean little; what does count is how much regular attention the hospitals and doctors give their patients.

Medical practitioners who actually work in or with rehabilitation centers frequently are there as precautionary devices and image enhancers. Their primary purpose usually is not the actual treatment of alcoholism but to watch for and care for other ailments that patients might get—particularly those resulting directly or indirectly from the institutions' regimens. That's the theory.

I have been in two centers that make much of their medical facilities. At both I was given cursory examinations by physician's assistants when I arrived. I was asked a few questions about my medical history, I was weighed, my blood pressure was taken, I was probed briefly with the usual ice-cold stethoscope, and had my knees banged with the inevitable rubber hammer—and that was it. In neither case did I ever meet the doctor in charge, nor did I see again the physician's assistants except in the dining halls. And I was in my sixties, which made me an old and vulnerable poop.

Actually, the medical care was non-existent as far as I could see, although both claimed to have staff doctors. In one, my long-standing advanced hypoglycemia was never checked, although I stressed it when I arrived. My blood pressure was taken two or three times, then ignored, though it was far too high. In the other center, my tussle with congestive heart failure was dismissed, and I wasn't even put on a low-salt diet—which I wouldn't have stuck to anyhow—but all the food was so bad that I happily lost more than twenty pounds in twenty-eight days, which wasn't even noticed.

My own personal doctor, an internist, later told me that one of these centers never got in touch with him for my medical background, though it had plenty of information and could have found him in the Washington telephone book.

I have a theory about the lack of medical attention. The doctors in rehabilitation centers, because of their environment, are often inclined to blame everything on alcoholism. One sweet old bum, admitted to a center where I was a patient, developed paralysis of the right arm. The center's doctor diagnosed it as "alcoholic arthritis." It got worse and eventually the patient was transferred to a regular hospital where he died a few days later. The "alcoholic arthritis" was a series of strokes.

Another patient had for many months been on oral medication for diabetes. In keeping with the center's no-pills policy, the medication was stopped after he arrived at the center. No diet was prescribed. Just before he successfully completed the course, a blood sugar reading was taken. His diabetes had progressed to the point where he had to take high-dose insulin shots every day.

It is helpful in soliciting funds and patients for rehabilitation center facilities to be able to advertise medical doctors on their staffs. It contributes not only to the prestige, but to an aura of safety. Sometimes the doctors have financial interests in the facilities, which may or may not make any difference. Certainly no organization could promote itself by advertising its staff as mostly non-drinking alcoholics, though insiders might realize that is a high recommendation.

So you just have to use your own judgment on how much secondary medical help should be available, perhaps with the help of your personal physician. Merely asking about it may bring more solicitude for the patient. It will be an indication that you are aware of the importance of medical supervision and the possibilities of malpractice complaints.

Drugs and Treatment

You should certainly explore the use of drugs in the centers. I have heard about, though not attended, centers that rely on drugs after detoxification to tranquilize the patients and to ease the severe depressions that often afflict alcoholics. Amphetamines and other uppers aren't unheard of, though their purpose is unclear and they can be hazardous.

With some notable exceptions, the most generally accepted therapy is drugless and relies heavily on the teachings of Alcoholics Anonymous. In the present stage of development in alcoholism treatment this would seem the most reliable framework. Even a good many centers that do use drugs often also teach and follow the tenets of AA.

One thing is certain: it is no great triumph to cure a patient of alcoholism by turning him into a Valium freak. The sole purpose of an alcoholism center should be to get the patients off alcohol—and drugs, if there is a cross addiction—not to create substitute addictions.

Here again you must use your own discretion, based on common sense, perhaps fortified by your doctor's views, and with consideration of the patient's character. If he has shown addictive tendencies, if he has had an unreasonable fondness for sleeping pills or tranquilizers or potent cough syrups or practically anything else except chewing gum and cigarettes, you had best play it safe. All this is oversimplified, of course, because again it all comes down to a matter of judgment.

Therapists' Backgrounds

You would want to know what sort of therapists the center has. One of the primary qualifications for a good therapist may well be drinking experience; a boozy past is considered good training. It provides not only a deeper understanding of the alcoholic and a sympathy for what he is going through, but a determination to save him if it possibly can be done. Yet a few of the best therapists I have known have never been even occasional drinkers.

Sundry Comforts

On the more practical side, you should inquire about living accommodations, transportation, laundry facilities, visiting schedules, the availability of a store where such things as cigarettes, razor blades, combs, sanitary napkins, and other incidentals can be purchased. Adequate facilities of this nature reduce the petty annoyances and distractions for which most new patients search constantly as justifications for their unhappiness and escape. Such things as candy bars, for example, assume a ridiculous importance, partly because the alcoholic deprived of his ethanol frequently has a tremendous craving to replace it with an appetizing form of sugar. Candy bars are an obvious choice. Some of the wretched versions of candy available in coin machines simply will not suffice.

A trip to the company store becomes an event in itself. The routine in a rehabilitation center can be so deadly that any diversion is welcomed. Some patients even enjoy doing their own laundry. At least it is something different.

On the matter of food: it may help to find out whether meals are prepared in the center's own kitchen or whether they are supplied by a big central feeding organization. If food is prepared on the premises, the patients at least have the satisfaction of knowing where to complain. If it is delivered from a mass-production kitchen, perhaps you can check on the caterer's reputation and be guided accordingly. Special diets usually are available for those who should not have salt and for diabetics. They will be just as good, or bad, all things considered, as the food in general. The question of kosher food would have to be checked specifically; a number of my fellow-patients were Jews, but so far as I know, none kept kosher.

As for sampling the food yourself—at most centers you can ease yourself into an invitation to eat, but it doesn't prove much. If the meal happens to be good— "that's the way it always is"; if it happens to be bad— "gosh, you certainly picked a bad day to eat here. Usually, it's pretty good." A somewhat more reliable indication of whether the food is tolerable can be had by asking other patients. They will usually have few qualms about being frank.

The Critical Questions

The jumbo questions you want answered, of course, are what does treatment cost and where will you get the money to pay the bill. Financing of treatment is, naturally, an overwhelming consideration to most people. Although there are no surefire rules, some guidelines on financing will be laid out later in this chapter.

Perhaps the second most persuasive factor will probably be what the place looks like. If the surroundings are depressing and forbidding, that is a big minus. If the collective attitude of the staff personnel seems friendly and interested, that is a big plus. Fancy decor means nothing either way. A spartan but cheerful atmosphere is probably good, since the purpose is not to supply luxury but education and treatment. And a center's general reputation, if you can judge it, also is of prime importance.

Apart from the question of cost, the final assessment of any treatment center is simple: does it work? In all likelihood you will find yourself heavily influenced by people who have gone through rehab centers and found them effective. This is fine; no better recommendation can be found. Usually, the phony centers can be spotted only through others' opinions, much like finding a good plumber or TV repairman.

With all these elements in mind, you should narrow the list to at least two options, to allow the patient himself a choice, if he is capable of it, and thus delude him into thinking he made the final decision. Such a process does more than merely soothe the patient's ego and lessen his suspicion that he is being railroaded; it also defuses the almost inevitable rebellion against the place in the early days of treatment, on the grounds that "this dump *you* sent me to stinks." You didn't pick it out—he did.

Packed and Ready to Go

Before the decisive shoot-out with the potential patient, a bag should be packed, or at least a list drawn up of what he should take. Such a precaution helps cut down last-minute arguments over whether he will need his special cue stick or custom-made bowling ball. It will speed up the business of hustling him off once he has agreed to go.

The list should include the usual clothes as required, with the omnipresent bathrobe, slippers, and pajamas. Comfortable shoes and ear plugs are musts; a transistor radio and a clock are usually welcome, along with a minimal supply of toiletries—minimal not only for convenience but because any live-in place occasionally will be afflicted not only with petty thievery but with free-loading colleagues who may appropriate anything they see.

THE STARTING LINEUP

Once the physical and financial preliminaries are completed comes the selection of the first team that will confront the potential patient. A minimum of two persuaders is preferable, not as a show of strength—although that can be handy if the patient becomes muscularly obstreperous, as sometimes happens. More to the point, two or more persuaders, between them, can better spot holes in a recalcitrant's defense and can better engulf him in reasons why he should take drastic action forthwith. But the attacking force should not be large, else it will clutter up things with too much verbiage, allow distraction through tangential arguments, and otherwise obscure the one and only aim of the discussion. Also, a big group may stiffen the alcoholic's resistance by dramatizing the fact that he is the victim of a gang-up.

A good selection would include two people, not necessarily professionals, with experience in handling alcoholics. Men and women who have done Twelfth Step work for Alcoholics Anonymous can anticipate and meet almost any ruse a drunk can invent. (The Twelfth Step says simply that Fellowship members, having had an awakening themselves, try "to carry this message to alcoholics. . . ." In other words, they try to help other alcoholics achieve sobriety. Twelfth Step workers usually are volunteers. Some have saved literally thousands.)

One of the two experts can be the rough and tough type, who fights with brass knuckles on his adjectives, who simply says "that's a lot of crap" when the drunk tries to deny or duck. The other should be more calm, more logical, more gentle. One or the other persuader should have some effect, depending upon the nature of the patient. One of the most successful Twelfth Steppers now in operation anywhere uses only the harsh approach; he had no luck whatever with me. The two young people who did get through used as their most forceful argument the simple question that if I had a broken leg or a kidney stone, I would go to an expert for help, wouldn't I? Since alcohol was my problem, I should go to an authority on alcoholism, shouldn't I? They had me.

Also in the group should be a trusted friend, a non-irritating relative, plus a spouse, if any. If they are alert and sympathetic, they can handle diversionary delaying stratagems that are beyond the ken of the frontline team, such as the target-patient insisting he must be around for spring planting, for his mother's summer visit, for the St. Patrick's Day parade, or to fix the roof before winter.

The friend and/or relative can also help refute the almost-certain insistence by the drunk that he does not need drastic help, that he can cut down or quit by himself. The veteran alcoholism helpers can customarily handle this issue best, but they sometimes need reinforcement.

How the group is brought together with the central figure is entirely up to the arrangements committee. But once it starts, it should be deadly serious. The alcoholic should realize the extreme gravity of the situation. There should be an absolute minimum of interruptions—no long telephone calls, no babies to feed, no visitors, no roasts in the oven, no stereos or television.

Scoring Points

The patient's reaction may be anything from anger to zeal. But almost certainly, he will insist he is not an alcoholic and will resent being considered one. Anger and denial are the two most common reflexes. It will become a fencing match. If the alcoholic has serious traffic charges pending, he must be told that a lawyer has been or will be consulted to arrange a hearing delay, and that the best defense would be the fact that the drunk is getting treatment. If he has high blood pressure or an arhythmic heart beat or arthritis, he must be told the doctor has been consulted, or will be, and that the patient probably will be better off physically during and after treatment. If he says he cannot be spared from his job right at this point, he must be told his boss is all for the plan and that the alcoholic may lose his job for good unless he snaps out of it. So it will go, on and on.

One woman I was involved in trying to salvage refused to budge, arguing that her daughter was launching a career in ballet and the mother's presence and support were essential. I talked to the daughter, and without prompting she forbade her mother to attend rehearsals or performance unless she got treatment and quit drinking.

Sometimes the rescue operations do not get the cooperation they need from others. A fairly high government official was in sufficiently bad shape to have his name pop up in gossip columns as being off-balance in bars and at formal dinners. His immediate boss told us the official would be fired if he did not change. We finally persuaded the official to accept treatment, and he needed only his boss's approval to have it financed by the office's health-care program. When the requisite papers reached the boss, however, he suddenly switched, decided he had faith in his alcoholic assistant, thought he could make it on his own and did not need treatment. What caused the reversal we have no idea, but we finally went over the head of the immediate superior and got the papers through. It meant weeks of turmoil and more gossipy society-column items.

In cases not initiated by the alcoholic's employer or supervisor, the question of whether to solicit his help can be agonizing, particularly if the boss is not known well by the husband or wife or relatives or friends who must make the decision. Even if he is known to the family, and considered to be objective and enlightened in most areas, he may have a deeply ingrained prejudice against alcoholism and alcoholics. About all the plotters can do is learn all they can about the boss in question, make a decision one way or the other, and hope.

There is no way scenarios can be planned for critical confrontations with an alcoholic. They must be extemporaneous because no one, not even the patient himself, knows what arguments will be made. The manipulators must be ready for anything and everything. And above all, they must make the alcoholic understand that this is it. If a husband or wife is involved, he or she must be convinced that, without treatment, this is the end of the marriage. If work is involved, the patient must have it burned into his mind that his job is at stake. If he is a politician or otherwise self-employed, he must get it through his spongy head that he is ruining his career.

All this is not as difficult as it sounds. A group that has lived with, and tolerated, an alcoholic should have the answers—the truth—right at the tip of its collective tongue.

Different Strokes

Such confrontations are not easy on any of the participants. The alcoholic perhaps suffers least, if only because his mind usually is not clear, he is protected by his alcoholic thinking, and he will feel self-righteously abused. Those who are trying to save him will approach him with a troubling mixture of affection and revulsion, of respect and scorn, of desperation and hopefulness. One feeling they must conceal, if they have it, is any desire for revenge for the unhappiness and discord the alcoholic has brought into their lives. The alcoholic seldom can admit he is responsible for these things, and any indication of getting even will tend to infuriate him and strengthen his obstinancy. He must be made to realize that the only motive for the meeting is to help him, while there is time and hope.

Different people have different philosophies about when to close in on the alcoholic in extremis. Some favor letting him reach absolute bottom, then rubbing his nose in it. They want to tell him in raw language that he is no good to anyone, including himself, that his life is an unmitigated mess, that no one has any more regard for him than he has for himself—which is usually none. Unless he will get help, either from AA or a rehabilitation center, he will simply continue to rot and nobody will give a damn.

Others are inclined toward tough supportiveness, stressing the positive—the good he will do for himself and consequently for those around him—if he will let the experts take him in hand, whether these experts be AA, a rehabilitation center, or a doctor of some kind who knows alcoholism.

And, of course, there are gradations of each approach. No one system can be considered all right or all wrong. Each will succeed or fail with different types of personalities; and considering the mercurial nature of alcoholics, different methods will have varying results at different times on the same person. Much of this has to be figured out while the confrontation is going on. Sometimes the approach will have to be abruptly changed in mid-discussion, which is another reason two experienced drunk-dealers should be on hand, each following a different course. When one course seems to be leading somewhere, the other will instinctively shut up.

Nagging Is Bad

One thing that almost never works is what I classify as nagging. It's a vague term, but under confrontational circumstances, I would think it covers the sometimes overpowering desire to tell an alcoholic all his comparatively petty faults and wrongdoings. He never helped with the dishes, he never changed a light bulb, he never mowed the lawn, he was late for dinner half the time, he spent far too much time and money drinking with the boys while the children had holes in their shoes. The field is unlimited. But the drunk can always remember times when he did help with the dishes, did change a light bulb, did mow the lawn and in his disoriented thinking he considers these exceptions the rule and proof that he gets credit for nothing good and blame for everything bad.

A full definition of what constitutes nagging would require an encyclopedic volume of its own. A nagger usually has no conscious realization he or she is nagging. So far as I know, there are only two ways to restrain a nagger; one is by keeping the conversation on the truly broad issues, such as overall damage to the marriage and the family, and the economic and social cost of drinking. The other is to have an objective person nearby who will kick the nagger in the shins when he or she starts.

The general atmosphere at one of these crucial meetings should be subdued. Reasonableness should be the key word. If there are angry shouts, crude and insulting remarks, harsh and unenforceable threats, let them come from the alcoholic. Once in a great while, a persuader can indulge in vehement language, but it should be done deliberately, without excessive passion. If used too much and too loudly, it loses its effectiveness.

DOUBLE TAKE

The confrontation, no matter how well managed, may not work immediately. It may not work at all. The alcoholic will almost certainly give up reluctantly. But the confrontation may galvanize his thinking processes, bring some order out of incoherence, make him realize dimly that he must act. If he is further prodded—directly but delicately—by his kin and colleagues, it may help. A major humiliation or mishap can do wonders. One well-known political figure who had been intractable in two confrontations was found one morning passed out in his car in a hotel parking lot in Washington. He was embarrassed and frightened by the gossip or headlines that might result. He was soon safely tucked away in a rehabilitation center. A not-so-well-known scientist in a similar situation pulled a death-defying stunt that is almost the trademark of an alcoholic—he fell asleep with a lighted cigarette in his hand. When the furor died down and his minor burns healed, he too got into line.

But if no such turnabout takes place, the interested parties should wait for a new degrading episode in the alcoholic's career, then pounce again. Maybe the alcoholic won't get the raise he had planned on, maybe his application for a new car loan will be turned down, maybe he won't be invited to participate this season in his bowling league, maybe any one of a thousand things. If he is sufficiently upset, another confrontation can be set up.

PREVENTION—KNOWN AS INTERVENTION

Most of what I've said about confrontation is based on the premise that you are dealing with a hardened alcoholic who has just about totalled himself. But another grade of drinker may need attention just as much. He is the extremely heavy drinker who does not quite meet the low but tough standards that mark the total alcoholic. He is sometimes called an alcohol "abuser," which is a description that has never rung quite right to me because the alcohol abuses him just as much as he abuses the alcohol. Besides, how do you abuse an alcohol? A child, a dog, a horse, yes—but alcohol?

Anyhow, trying to stop a heavy drinker before he reaches bottom is more difficult and more uncertain. For one thing, he can make a much more logical argument that he is not powerless over alcohol and his life has not become unmanageable. For another, he very likely has not experienced the physical and mental torment of a true alcoholic. He is probably still in the relatively fun stage of drinking and is not doing obvious damage (that he can recognize, at least), so why give it up?

Working with such a character is further complicated by the fact that some drinkers can be "abusers" for years before they become alcoholics, if indeed they ever do; others are abusers for a very short time before alcohol becomes an addiction rather than a lark. Efforts to prevent abusers from becoming alcoholics are often called "interventions" and are getting more and more attention. Certainly they are worthwhile; avoiding devastating tragedy is far better than trying to pick up the pieces afterwards.

In an intervention session, the central figure must be made to realize, if possible, that the pleasant lane he currently is following will almost certainly become, sooner or later, the rocky road of alcoholism, leading only to horror and ruin.

The first goal of an intervention is to pierce the thick membrane of alcoholic thinking in which the drunk is encased. Then he must be persuaded the situation is extremely grave; much damage has already been done, more will be done, unless the situation changes. He must be made to realize that nobody is fabricating these ideas; they are detailed only because people are genuinely concerned. He must be persuaded to consider that sobriety can actually be more enjoyable than drunkenness, that alcohol is not an essential ballast to sail the turbulent seas of life. Then he must be prevailed upon to make a serious attempt at quitting through Alcoholics Anonymous, by going to a counselor, by becoming an out-patient in a counseling program or by going to a rehabilitation center.

Intervention is frequently attempted by the same people who produce confrontations—families, friends, coworkers, and AA. But they are sometimes most successful when job-related. I will go into that later in connection with labor-management alcoholism programs, which could become one of the most important developments in years in efforts to control the disease.

WHERE'S THE MONEY COMING FROM???

The problem of paying for the treatment I deliberately left to now, not only because it is complicated, vague, and varied but because it is imperative that both the alcoholic and those who would help understand the enormity of the situation. If the patient had a classifiable illness, such as cancer or a worn-out heart or a ruptured appendix or a bullet wound, he and you would think first of adequate treatment and second of the money to meet the bills. Alcoholism should be in the same category. But I cannot count the number of times I have been told, "He can't possibly go to one of those places—we simply don't have the money." Money can be a ghastly obstacle.

The first step is to check whatever health insurance the patient has, if any. Policies and practices vary widely but more and more policies are covering alcoholic treatment in approved institutions, partly as a result of initiatives taken by both management and unions. If the patient is covered by health insurance, the rehabilitation institution selected must be one that accepts such insurance, and is itself accepted by the insurance company.

The number of people covered by major medical—health insurance for serious illnesses rather than runny noses, diarrhea, and headaches—was to me astonishing. At the time I checked, the Health Insurance Association of American put the figure at 147,555,000. It has increased surprisingly over the past two years, perhaps largely because labor unions have realized that since such benefits are not taxable, they are often preferable to pay increases. Also, as medical and hospital costs climb, the health benefits themselves become more valuable. Without insurance, one major medical problem can wipe out a family, in an economic sense. In addition, insurance companies gradually are becoming aware of the fact that they save money by reducing alcoholism rather than paying for the results of alcoholism—prolonged sicknesses, traffic and industrial accidents, and so on.

Probably a majority of the major medical policies cover treatment for alcoholism. I was told by experts in the field that "most" do. Generally, the decision is up to the employee or his union or both. In the federal government and in many or most labor union contracts, the employee is offered his choice of several different types of policies. The more extensive the coverage, the more a policy may cost. It was interesting to me that employees are inclined to pick the more expensive policies with the widest coverage. Presumably, most people figure the difference is small when divided into months or weeks or even days— and it could prevent a great deal of economic hardship.

Most of the policies are deductible—the patient himself must pay the first $100 or $200 or more of the cost of treatment. The insurance then will cover perhaps 80 percent of the rest. Policies covering alcoholism are not always more costly. As a matter of fact, spokesmen for the Kemper Group, which describes itself as "a major diversified insurance and financial services organization," contend it might well cost less by reducing subsequent claims. The Kemper Group was a real pioneer in rating alcoholism as a treatable disease. It began including alcoholism in some policies in 1964, as did Wasau, long before statistics were available to support the action. The latest estimates I have found show that perhaps 700 companies and about 70 Blue Cross programs provided alcoholism coverage in 1980.

The coverage theoretically is cost-effective by reducing expenditures for later illnesses and accidents resulting from alcoholism; some statistics indicate that 15 out of 100 health-insurance claims are tied in somehow with alcoholism, as are four out of every ten industrial accidents.

Then there are traffic injuries and deaths, about half of which are reckoned to involve alcohol in some fashion.

The moral of all this is that you should check your health insurance, both before and after alcoholism strikes. Check before because it is impossible to predict where or when alcoholism will hit. However remote such a tragedy may seem, you should be protected. One woman with whom I talked actually had lived with her husband for 22 years—in what she thought was a glorious marriage—when he suddenly admitted he was an advanced alcoholic. His wife absolutely did not know, never even suspected he had more than a token highball at a party. He asked for help and spent months in a hospital and in rehabilitation.

If treatment is not covered by insurance, one important point must be considered when digging around for alternative financing: many, perhaps most, reputable care centers allow delayed payment. Eighteen months seems a common period. Some want regular installments but exceptions are made. A substantial down payment is almost always required. The lowest I found was 20 percent—a fifth. There may be some lower, and obviously many are higher—running up to 50 percent. Normally to get a deferred-payment plan, the applicant must get a credit clearance. The standards for credit clearance obviously will vary widely from center to center, but generally they are not as severe as one might expect in view of the fact that few drunks even remember to pay back that five bucks they borrowed to tide them over to payday. While the commercial care centers are obviously trying to make money, they also want to help alcoholics. They may be inclined to bend, at least a little, even in cases where regular commercial companies would summarily reject a credit application. If they don't they probably are not worth bothering with anyhow.

Also, some rehabilitation centers have what are almost-secret help programs for the destitute; so far as I know, such aid usually is available only in nonprofit care centers financed through fees and by gifts and endowments. The funds are not ballyhooed because the whole idea is to hold them as last resorts in truly desperate cases.

A union or a fraternal organization may have special funds to help families of members facing severe medical emergencies, which may well include alcoholism. Point out, of course, that the situation is critical. Sometimes the union or the lodge can pick up the tab if the patient technically is committed, not for alcoholism, but for one or more of the symptoms—inflamed liver, pancreatitis, heart failure or whatever. The same device can be used with some health insurance programs and with Health Maintenance Organizations—HMOs.

Any suggestions here need not be followed in rotation. Logically, you first try avenues you feel, in your case, are most likely to lead somewhere. A number of people I know have gone directly to banks or credit unions, sometimes without disclosing the real purpose of the loans. Others have talked with social workers and welfare officials and found their states, or occasionally communities, have help tucked away in odd corners.

Other measures I have known people to take involve a second mortgage on a home, sale of the family car, and even a yard sale (or garage sale or whatever it is called in your vicinity). One of these informal flea markets pulled in an astonishing $3,200, but it also created a few minor problems; the new family ironing board and microwave oven were sold at less than the family had just paid for them.

Again, one of the good potential sources of guidance in some localities is the nearest affiliated office of the National Council on Alcoholism. The names of the affiliated offices are different in different localities. They are listed in Appendix I of this book.

Finally there is the possibility of commitment to a state institution. In a few states, they are uniformly good. In others, they will be good one year and bad the next, depending upon the political climate. In perhaps a majority of states, they should be avoided with all the determination and dexterity you can manage. One problem is that many of them lump alcoholics together with extreme psychiatric cases, where the alcoholic obviously cannot get anything resembling the type of attention he needs.

Finding the money will be a scramble, with disappointments and humiliations aplenty. But anyone who starts what can become a downright frantic search for assistance can probably find sources that I overlooked or don't know about. During the whole messy business, one consideration must dominate your actions: you are dealing with a dangerous, perhaps critical, medical problem.

Only one thing is fairly certain when you start out to keep a mulish or incipient drunk from self-destructing; it won't be easy and it won't go smoothly for either side. But emotional concern, tinted with ego and practical considerations, will keep you going; propelling the drunk will be his own misery, along with remnants of pride, common sense and affection for those around him.

Both sides will need luck.

8

Those Eggs
Are Fragile

Let us suppose that all the tortuous problems have been unravelled, our drunk has finished the prescribed treatment and it seems to have worked; it happens more often than is reasonable, considering the difficulties.

But also more often than you might think, it is wiped out after he is through by the clumsiness of the very people who struggled to help him in the first place. Every whit as important as getting a person into treatment is the subsequent process known as "aftercare," a term that has, for me, vaguely unpleasant connotations.

The family and friends of the patient should consider what they have on their hands. The patient is dry but not necessarily sober. The alcohol is gone from his system but the desire for it probably is not. Two or four or six weeks is long enough to get it out of the blood but not out of the mind.

The fact that he knows or suspects he still wants a drink can contribute to uneasiness. He has sentenced himself never to have another drink but he isn't sure he can stick it out. He is not even sure he wants to.

He knows a great deal about himself that he didn't know before. He has come eyeball to eyeball with at least some of his shortcomings, his faults, his failures. These he wants to correct. He has renewed his own hope and the hopes of those who want him to make it. But he wonders whether he is strong enough to fulfill those hopes. Or will he flop again? This uncertainty kept me on edge for months and I was not sure enough of myself to face up to my own misgivings.

Often this turmoil is very much inner. Customarily, the afflicted will seem relaxed and happy, and in a sense he is, because he knows he has the best chance so far to get that big ugly monkey off his back. But the doubts are more troublesome because of his alcoholic thinking. He can't quite sort things out, can't quite make everything fit. In other words, he may be in mental turmoil. Not as much as when he was drunk, but far from the serene state he may seem to have reached.

In my own case, my 90-proof thinking would flare up every now and then for at least eighteen months after I had "achieved sobriety," as they say in AA. I suddenly became aware that a personal liaison that could conceivably have resulted in remarriage was downright grotesque. Also, I almost loused up two business deals in ways that would have made my wobbly future even more chaotic. And I was, on several occasions, petulantly paranoid about people who had made the greatest sacrifices to help me when I seemed beyond help. Thanks to the kindly beatings I had taken at clinics, and to the pervasive support I got from Alcoholics Anonymous, I got by, I think.

It is the fear of sneaky outbursts of cockeyed thinking that prompt wise counselors to advise a patient to make no major decisions in his life—marrying, divorcing, quitting his job, selling the family homestead, or buying a summer place in Sri Lanka—for at least a year, except, of course, when the therapists agree that some such drastic action is an imperative part of the treatment.

A recovering alcoholic soon learns to recognize, understand, and subdue alcoholic thinking when it does pop up. As a matter of fact, the recovering alcoholic can be considered excellent material for most everything—for employment, for companionship, for marriage, for breeding. In reaching sobriety, he has learned a great deal about himself and others. He knows his shortcomings better than most. He is more honest with himself. The lessons he has absorbed often make him kinder and more gentle than some of his more upright associates.

I do not, however, advocate becoming a drunkard to better oneself. There are easier ways.

An awareness of what may be going on in the thought processes of a dry alcoholic is handy in trying to make him a sober alcoholic. And at least some of the things I've mentioned almost certainly will be among the emotions with which any dry drunk must wrestle. He hopes he is a new person; he is trying to be a new person; and he must be treated as a new person. He should not be babied; it's his fight. Neither should he be shamed; the things he did that were shameful happened in his previous life, when he was very, very sick.

He should never forget these shameful things, but neither should he brood over them. The fact that they were brought on by an avoidable illness will not justify letting them happen again. But neither should it engender a pervading guilt that can jeopardize a normal existence.

Reminding a recovering alcoholic of his past usually should be avoided. If others remind him of what he was, he instinctively may think he will be judged forever on the basis of the past rather than the present. If he will continue to be considered a drunk, he might as well be a drunk; so he may reason.

It is far better to let him do the talking about his drinking days and if his recovery is progressing well, he probably will. His inclination to hide his background, to be ashamed of it, should become less and less; his openness about it will be to him a cathartic, a matter of pride, and a hope that such an attitude may give a boost to other unfortunates with the disease.

Whether a recovering alcoholic discloses his background to a potential employer when he is looking for a job is a determination he alone can make. If there is a chance the employer will find out anyhow, the alcoholic should be completely frank, and show pride rather than shame. If his past is unlikely to be exhumed, the question should be given some thought. If an employer is himself a heavy drinker, he may take a dim view of a teetotaller, for fear it may put him in a bad light. And there is always the person who thinks alcoholism is an unpardonable sin. Generally, however, a confession that the alcoholic had a problem but now has it under control will elevate him in the opinion of an enlightened employer.

He should be encouraged to talk about things that bother him—his home and sex life, his children, finances, his misgivings about himself, others' faults, his job, concerns about the future. Dispassionate discussions of these sorts can be very helpful to all concerned.

Without being coddled, he must be reinforced in his resolve in every possible way. He must be treated with respect but not subservience, with dignity but not with coldness, with thoughtfulness but not as royalty. Above all, he must not be ridiculed. What he's been through—and put others through—may stimulate many different responses, but ridicule must not be one of them.

He may joke about himself. Many renovated drunks do, to the point of boredom. But if anyone else tries it, the resentment may be powerful.

The way recovering alcoholics are handled sometimes can be downright evil. One older man I knew was constantly bedeviled by his wife for what she insisted was irresponsible behavior. He was a heavy drinker, probably an alcoholic, so at the insistence of his peers he volunteered to go to a rehabilitation center in which I was a patient. His wife then moved swiftly; working with two cooperative doctors who knew she had partial control of the family money, she had him committed to a psychiatric hospital as a manic-depressive. With expert legal help, he got out in a month and entered the alcoholism clinic, where his wife visited him and the clinic therapists every few days to insist he was insane, not an alcoholic.

Before it was over, the therapists bluntly told the patient and his wife that, in their estimation, she didn't want him "cured"; she just wanted him out of the way.

Anyhow, when he completed the rehabilitation course, he was doing very well indeed. But never did his wife stop telling him he was nuts. Under the incessant barrage, his determination was fading fast. He filed for divorce, which she fought for years and may still be fighting. At a court hearing the fact came out that if he were forcibly exiled to a mental institution she would get unqualified control over all the family funds, which were considerable.

Mishandling a recovering alcoholic usually is the result of ignorance rather than avarice. For example, one wife bragged to me of always smelling her husband's breath when he returned from work, or golf, or the store, to make sure he hadn't been sneaking drinks. A husband assured me that his wife was doing excellently after treatment; he knew, because he surreptitiously called her friends regularly to check on whether she had been drinking and he periodically searched the house for hidden bottles.

Casual cracks can be just as devastating as such overt demonstrations of lack of confidence. Even my own wife, who was one of the most understanding, tactful people I have ever known, could goof. I called her after a couple of weeks in my first rehabilitation course, to tell her that for the first time in years I didn't need or want a drink. Her response was a jovial, "well, it's about time."

It sounds trivial and under ordinary circumstances it would have been. But at that particular point, I needed a lift, a suggestion that she was surprised, relieved, pleased, and even proud; what I distinctly did not need was a reminder of how stupid I had been for so long. I was dashed but fortunately feeling sufficiently mellow so I simply laughed and said something to the effect that "now you are the one that has to learn a few things." It was the only mistake she made.

SOME GROUND RULES

Alcoholics' aftercare reactions are predictably diverse. Handling them is largely a matter of common sense and insight. But there are fundamental ground rules that should be considered. Rehabilitation centers that follow the teachings of Alcoholics Anonymous almost invariably stress, as Rule One, attendance at AA meetings. I have already explored the incalculable value of AA in maintaining the dryness that should subsequently become sobriety. It can be so great that sometimes it will accomplish what the center itself fell short of doing. One rehab clinic that I consider verging on the fraudulent has a moderately respectable record of achievement for one reason alone: every night of the week, it shepherds its patients to outside AA meetings. The patients, without exception, either have previously rejected AA or have not responded to its pitch. But steady exposure for four to eight weeks, although forced, works wonders. The patients could do this themselves—without paying the center the thousands of dollars their course costs—but they have shown they won't.

Many rehab places have their own aftercare setups, some of which are effective. At the minimum, they will give the patient names of AA members to call in his area, to find a sponsor, a list of meetings, and any other guidance he may need. They also probably will politely bedevil the patient to make sure he goes to meetings. They will usually try to avoid being nuisances but they can be persistent, because they take a deep interest in preventing a relapse.

If a patient resists AA at this stage, any device can be tried to break him down. Perhaps a good friend can be enlisted to act as escort, instead of or in company with the assigned sponsor. In two cases I know of, the bartenders at the patients' regular drinking spots went with their former customers until the patients got into the habit and realized they were profiting from AA. In another instance, the owner of a saloon took over the task although, as he himself put it, his efforts would probably result in his bankruptcy, since the patient had been a fabulous customer.

Non-alcoholic family members can accompany a patient to open meetings and can be valuable in supplying spiritual support and in giving respectability to the sobering process. There are all sorts of possibilities. One lawyer enticed a reluctant alcoholic to take him—the lawyer—to AA meetings. The lawyer's bait was legitimate; he said he had to handle so many cases involving drunks that he wanted to know what made them tick. And a judge interested in alternative sentencing—the sentencing of offenders to rehabilitation and public-service work rather than prison—used the same honest logic on two of his friends.

Another standard regulation for aftercare patients is the avoidance of old haunts and old drinking companions. This often comes hard. The corner saloon sometimes has been, not a second home, but a first; it is frequently a haven for the alcoholic. And too often, the only friends he has are his barroom buddies.

This dilemma can be met by making the non-drinking environment as pleasant as possible. The home, or wherever the patient lives, should be free of tension and niggling annoyances. And the patient should be quietly encouraged to resume the avocations he has always seemed to find interesting but been too distracted to pursue. Maybe he is a repressed do-it-yourselfer; maybe he likes woodworking, or gardening, or tinkering with the car. Anything of this sort should be stimulated by proper appreciation and admiration.

In other words, as with a contrary child, suggest something else. It can go beyond the house; diversions can take in golf or tennis or birdwatching or movies or the theater or concerts or picnics or anything. The purpose is to keep the atmosphere pleasant and the alcoholic busy.

Until the patient regains his strength, in a manner of speaking, it probably is wise to have no liquor around the house; others around the place, whether visitors or residents, probably should not drink. Sometimes the patient will insist that alcohol be available on a business-as-usual basis, to test his own contempt for the stuff. But usually this period is not reached for weeks or months or maybe never. In my own case, I promised myself never again to have a bottle of booze sitting around the place because I felt that if I took one good swallow, I would finish the bottle and again go lurching down the path to oblivion. But after about a year of not being able to keep guests happy, I suddenly realized it didn't make a dime's worth of difference to me so I stocked up. Most of what I bought still sits on the shelf.

Some of those who come to see me, however, do drink reasonably so there is some attrition in my stock. And I have found several times that when a bottle is left out, unopened, the whiskey evaporates with incredible swiftness. Finally I realized that some of my friends who proclaimed most loudly that they had followed my example and given up the stuff, were sneaking drinks when I went to the bathroom or got tied up on the phone or was otherwise occupied. They undoubtedly reckoned that, with my new disregard for alcohol, I would never notice. Such is the surreptitious swiller's mentality: never drink a bottle totally empty, always allow just enough to cover the bottom of the jug.

As for husbands and/or wives continuing moderate drinking when around a recovering spouse—sometimes it is harmless, more often it does a great deal of damage. One particular friend, who drinks little and wisely, found his wife had become an alcoholic. He was quite prominent nationally, soaked with formal education and distinguished in his profession. But he was acutely ashamed of his wife's condition. In great secrecy, he got her into a hospital for treatment and she responded quite well. After several weeks, she was released and a few days later she and her husband gave a small, quiet party. Not a word had been said of her problem, but at the party it was not other guests who pushed drinks on her—but her own husband. I could see her struggle with herself each time he offered her a drink—urged her to have one. Each time the bourbon won. In three weeks, she was again a basket case. It happens far too often, whether from ignorance or malice who can say?

CALLING A HALT

Professional therapists have an acronym for how a recovering alcoholic should help himself. It is HALT. It means an alcoholic should avoid becoming Hungry, Angry, Lonely or Tired (or Tempted).

Hunger can be a sneaky trap. Few of us, alcoholics or not, have not succumbed to the lure of a beer or a drink of some sort while we waited, with whining stomachs, for food. Alcohol does give a momentary sense of energy, whether because of its quickly burned calories or its psychological jolt. But it won't genuinely satisfy hunger, although it may deaden the appetite; alcoholics are often badly undernourished, and when they stop drinking they frequently manifest intense cravings for candy and orange juice and other fast-acting forms of sugar. This is one reason the quality of food at a rehabilitation center is important. Special emphasis should be put on desserts. They need not be outlandishly large but they should be good.

A heavy drinker can lose weight, sometimes alarmingly, when he's on a binge. He probably eats very little, actually may be seriously undernourished. He consumes an enormous number of calories but the calories in alcohol do not come to rest as fat; they are burned up, often giving an illusion of energy. Also, they supply almost no nutrition, and in the long run, they depress rather than stimulate. Probably most of us have known people who drink their lunches or dinners. They confine themselves to diets of alcohol, using the excuse that they are trying to lose weight. They may indeed lose weight. They can lose a lot of other things, including their lives.

As for anger—it's the old nonsense of needing a drink to calm nerves or to quiet down or to cool off. Actually alcohol is a relaxant, of a sort. But because of its affect on the thinking processes, it can and does distort and magnify the original cause of the anger. An angry drinker, far from calming down, usually gets angrier with each slug. What may seem in perspective a minor irritation can be enlarged in his mind to a major incident and can encompass even innocent bystanders. The process somtimes ends only when the angry man passes out, or gets knocked out in a barroom brawl.

Sometimes the angry drinker will gradually become choked-up, not with belligerence, but with self-pity. Then we have the weeping drunk. But there is no way alcohol can alleviate rage; only time and logical thinking will do that. In the area of alcoholism, control of unjustifiable temper outbursts comes with sobriety unless other mental screw-ups are involved.

Loneliness is, to me, one of the most prevalent provocations for renewed drinking, as well as perhaps the most dangerous. Many, maybe most, recovering alcoholics have lost large numbers of their professional and social friends. They have only those who joined them in elbow-bending ballets at the bar and not only are these pals off-limits, but they don't usually accept abstinent buddies anyhow.

I was lucky. Most of my non-professional friends drank temperately or not at all. Some I hadn't seen much of, because they found my boozing distasteful and I found their sobriety disturbing. I made no secret of my "reformation," but neither did I trumpet it. I let my friends find out gradually, mostly by word of mouth. It didn't take long because the people I new were so astonished at the information that they couldn't keep it to themselves.

Most of the friends I valued forgave me for my past, largely on the basis of the death of my wife, which was charitable of them—and that I say with no snide implications. I was an alcoholic before my wife died; as I've said, her death was a peachy excuse to resume, but not an acceptable reason.

A very few of my friends could not go back to old intimacies; they could not forget the drunk; they think, consciously or otherwise, that the drinker was the real me, and that the sobriety provides a facade.

But as word of my condition seeped around, it did produce an effective remedy for my loneliness. Both old friends and remote acquaintances, startled at what had happened to me, began appealing to me for advice on how they could handle the alcoholic difficulties they confronted. The idea seemed to be that if I could get off alcohol, anybody could.

Sometimes the appeals involved the friends, their families or fellow-workers, occasionally the appellant himself. I became absorbed with trying to help when I could. My success rate was not phenomenal but it kept me busy. I did not do Twelfth Step work through Alcoholics Anonymous for a variety of reasons, but the personal calls fortified my own efforts to stay out of trouble.

Alcoholics Anonymous also was a great help in the loneliness department. Four nights a week it gave me somewhere specific to go, where I would meet nice people who understood what I was going through. My sponsor was nimble-witted and fun to be with; her husband was delightful. I hope they are still among my best friends. Incidentally, a sponsor is usually of the same gender as the patient, but I had the distinct impression that my original AA contacts couldn't find a man with sufficient courage to take me on.

Some AA activists base almost their entire social lives on AA, and it's not a bad deal. In the fellowship you find interesting companions, always some with interests parallel to yours, who are sympathetic to your position because they are there themselves. And you can be sure you will not be regarded as a freak because you prefer coffee. You can become as deeply involved in AA as you wish, and do yourself and others a great deal of good.

Another substitute for the saloon-oriented social life sometimes can be provided by keeping track of your classmates at a rehabilitation center. It is a great morale booster to get visits or phone calls from the people with whom you sweated it out—and to make calls to them. To the super-sophisticate, it may sound cornball, but you'd be surprised. Your former fellow-patients probably will often need help in staying on dry land and you can supply it; you yourself may need help, and they can supply it.

The final admonition—to avoid excessive tiredness or temptation—sounds imprecise, but it isn't. When an alcoholic comrade is totally wiped-out and feels only a drink will restore him, he should first resort to candy, pastry, a soft drink, or fruit—something with sugar; if this is forbidden, as in a diabetic, fruit is still probably acceptable and other edibles and drinkables will suffice. The effect will be the same, and a lot longer lasting, unless psychological influences are allowed to dominate. An alcoholic, or those around him, should always have enticing food available, whether it be ripe olives, smoked Canadian trout, or junk food from a coin machine. If worst comes to worst, the drunk must simply fight it through.

The obvious temptations to be avoided are, of course, visits to old hangouts and with old boozy friends. An additional item of assistance can be a list, either mental or written, of the circumstances under which the patient would feel the strongest urge for booze. The more common entries on such a list include cocktail parties, long automobile trips, dates with coveted males/females, boring receptions, and dull chamber music recitals.

In my own case, I was deathly afraid of two situations; one was a long plane ride in first class, where drinks are plentiful and free. The other was preceding and during what I expected to be a heavenly meal at a heavenly restaurant with heavenly people.

I could not, for the life of me, imagine flying from Washington to Hawaii, or from Kinshasa to New York, without an alcoholic escape, particularly since the environment seemed just right and custom dictated drinking. I had become thoroughly accustomed to such patterns when most of my traveling was done on expense accounts and luxury was routine.

Nor could I conceive of a particularly seductive meal without a cocktail and wine, and perhaps a brandy afterwards. I was convinced it would be as uncomfortable as dressing without underwear.

As soon as I felt I had a reasonably good grip on myself, I took a trip across the country and ate at my favorite San Francisco restaurant with congenial companions. On the plane, I discovered the thrill of being conscious of where I was going and what was happening; at dinner, I found flavors in the food that I had never known were there. I passed the test, with intensified pleasure.

One of the minor annoyances at a restaurant can be the haughty maitre d' or waiter whose scorn is apparent when you do not have a drink or wine. He looks at you as though you were a savage. It helps if you remind yourself that the profit margin on drinks, particularly wine, is usually large and sometimes extortionate, and the bigger the tab, the bigger the tip.

Poisonous people in general are a hazard as well as an irritant. One of the worst is the loud-mouthed intellectual ape, the drink pusher, who insists the alcoholic have a slug. He often becomes loud and offensive. "Aw c'm on, have one. Don't be a prude. Join the fun. Don't be a party pooper." You've all heard them, maybe even been one.

Equally assinine but not so noisy is the drink spiker who secretly slips booze into the alcoholic's Coke, "just to see what will happen." As a rule, the alcoholic will spot the trick, but not always. The spiker thinks it's funny.

Also nauseating are the lives of the party who boisterously, and they think humorously, rib the recovering alcoholic for his abstemiousness. Usually the ribbers or kidders are swacked themselves.

If you are female you must be wary of the person who

tries to load you up for the specific purpose of getting you into bed. Come to think of it, there should be no sexual discrimination in that statement. It's a ploy that doesn't often work unless the victim is predisposed to cooperate and even if it does work, the alcohol itself can interfere with an efficient and memorable result.

All these people the recovering alcoholic should try to avoid, and he should get the maximum cooperation from those around him.

BEWARE OF DRUGS

Still another area of caution involves the use of drugs. Many totally sober alcoholics have pathological scars from their drinking and drugs can have unpredictable consequences. I once loved the effect of so-called uppers, particularly amphetamines, but I was not addicted, physically or psychologically. Some of my better writing was done by virtue of Dexedrine, and later amphetamines. The drugs were perfectly legal then, and meaningful restrictions on prescriptions did not begin until after I had stopped their use entirely on my own volition. I wouldn't touch one now; heaven only knows what it would do to my unpickled carcass. In any event, letting an alcoholic play around with drugs can set him up for trouble.

Many alcoholics are believed to have addictive personalities or addictive tendencies. It means simply that they can be hooked more easily than the majority of people. Their addictive tendencies showed up in their alcoholism, and there is a good chance they might reappear with other substances, from eclairs to tomato catsup.

Every alcoholic, no matter how little or how much he is recovered, should explain fully his history to his doctor and his dentist. The dentist should be included because he might give the patient a prescription pain killer of a strength and in a quantity that would be little risk for most patients but might start another addiction in an alcoholic.

I have heard hair-raising stories of alcoholics' problems resulting from failure to inform doctors of their illness. Even when the doctor and dentist are alerted there is some risk because neither is necessarily fully aware of the potential hazards. Even stringent weight-loss or exercise programs should not be undertaken without the doctor having a full understanding of the patient's condition.

Sometimes drugs are part of the treatment for alcoholism. Perhaps the most generally known is antabuse. It causes the body to become thoroughly antagonistic to alcohol in any form. Anyone taking antabuse or a similar drug can, and usually does, become violently ill if he consumes even a tiny amount of alcohol. Use of the drug is, of course, based on the theory that if you know a drink will make you sick as a mule, you won't take it. But again, fear frequently is not enough. A close friend at one of the rehabilitation centers I went through voluntarily went on antabuse although he seemed to be well on his way to sobriety without it. All went fine for two or three months, then he succumbed to his friends' gurgling enjoyment of steins of cold beer and had one himself. He was in the hospital for six weeks.

Others have told me of becoming very ill just from smelling a cologne with a heavy alcohol content, or from eating a dessert flavored with rum. A young, successful entrepreneur in the catering business was to do a dinner I was to attend. She was planning a main dish and a dessert that included alcoholic ingredients; she knew my history, was worried and called Alcoholics Anonymous to ask whether the dishes would be safe. AA told her she should not take the chance—that the alcohol might get me started again and she could not be sure none of the guests was on antabuse. It would have made no difference to me, and the other guests drank like elephants, but the caterer's action demonstrated rare wisdom. She now checks routinely with the hosts or hostesses.

With some recovering alcoholics it takes very little to cause a relapse, according to the alcoholics themselves. Stories are rampant of people triggered by the skimpiest encounter with alcohol—eating a piece of Christmas fruit cake soaked in brandy, drinking water out of an unwashed glass that had held wine, or sitting in front of someone at the theater who had a beer-laden breath. Those who tell of such experiences swear they happened and they are possible. Most genuine recovering drunks, however, are not set on such hair triggers. One actual drink can do a lot of damage but succumbing to faint traces of alcohol is another matter.

When an alcoholic does have what is known as a "slip" in the jargon of sobriety, the alcoholic himself and those around him should move swiftly. If the skid lasts more than a few days, or a couple of months at the most, the drinker is in real danger. Even if the alcoholic does act quickly, he can have a monumental struggle with himself. He may be able to straighten out on his own; he may need increased exposure to, and pressure from, Alcoholics Anonymous; he may have to go back to a rehabilitation center.

As I have said, having been given the works once and earned his Bachelor of Sobriety degree, he should be more amenable to treatment than he was the first time around. Also, he knows he can do without liquor and he should be convinced he cannot play around with it; a skid should eliminate entirely any hidden hopes he could be a controlled drinker.

That's the way it works in most cases, but not all. A teenage alcoholic girl I know about got straightened out successfully, resisted peer pressure and every other kind for seven years. Yet almost overnight she once again became a sloppy, saturated drunk. The last I heard nothing had helped.

All this, you say, is a lot of trouble to take for one lousy drunk. Perhaps it is. It means you have to be a courteous, considerate, thoughtful human being in handling the drunk. If that is too much effort and strain, heaven help him and you. The recovering alcoholic is not bedridden, he can take care of himself physically, he is likely to be more pleasant, more useful, more stimulating and more fun than he ever was before. And most gratifying, you can watch him get better, rather than deteriorate and die. If it works, you will find it one of the most gratifying experiences of your life.

9

Meddling Can Be Profitable

The most erudite computer would vaporize if asked to estimate the savings in human misery were alcoholism to be eliminated. But properly programmed, it would scarcely bat a light if asked to measure the savings in money. The answer would not be dogmatically exact, but it would be close and run into the billions of dollars. Billions.

Several years ago, the federal department then known as Health, Education, and Welfare reported "alcoholic abuse and alcoholism drain the economy of an estimated $15 billion a year. Of this total, $10 billion is attributable to lost work time in business, industry, civilian government, and the military."

More recently the National Council on Alcoholism has set the figure at nearly $43 billion a year. Other figures go up to $60 billion. Considering how many people get away with alcoholic drinking, as I did for some time, I think the original HEW figure was far too low. And then there is inflation.

The National Council on Alcoholism's figures may take in more; they include not only poor job performance and absenteeism, but health and welfare services, property damage caused by befuddled brains, and medical expenses. Lost production alone, says the NCA, "has been computed at $19.64 billion annually." Just who or what computed the figure, and how, is not quite clear and neither can the amount be guaranteed correct. It does, however, appear reasonable; it seems obvious that the 6 to 10 percent of the workers at all levels who are alcoholics cannot possibly contribute as much to the national economy as they cost it.

Business in general is caught in a crack. The first impulsive reaction usually is to fire the employee whose work deteriorates because of excessive drinking. But it is a savage solution and a waste in human resources, just as it would be to fire those who get any other treatable disease. That's why we have health-care programs—to save people and manpower.

A more acceptable solution, which has pretty well proven itself, comes under the general heading of "intervention." In this instance, it means carefully structured joint labor-management programs to prevent and cut down occupational alcoholism.

I became intensely curious about intervention programs during my first go-round with a rehabilitation clinic. I found that about one third of the patients were there because they had been told by their bosses to get treatment or lose their jobs; those who belonged to unions had been told, in addition, that their shop stewards and locals for once agreed with the bosses.

One such fellow-sufferer came into the place simply choking with indignation. He was a steelworker who had a good hard hat supervisory job. He had committed no crimes, but his work had become exceedingly sloppy—

according to his bosses. After the customary few days of adjustment, he began unloading his anger at therapy sessions.

- He was not an alcoholic, never drank on the job.
- His drinking was none of the company's business; it was strictly a private matter and the company had no right to interfere.
- His immediate boss was gunning for him because he wouldn't kiss-ass but insisted on his rights.
- His boss's attitude created such tension that the employee was driven to drink.
- That goddamned union was a bunch of finks who had sold out to management. After all the money he had paid in dues, and in spite of what he considered faithful attendance at meetings, the union refused to lift a finger when he was in trouble.
- He had given the best years of his life to the company and to the union, and this was the thanks he got—railroaded, on trumped-up charges.

He had much more to blow off but this is an adequate sample. He was convinced everything he said was true. Then his patient-colleagues, who had been in the program perhaps five or ten days longer than he, began asking questions. How much did he drink? Mostly on weekends. Never during the week? Sometimes a couple of shots before bed because he had trouble sleeping; finally, his total reached somewhat less than a quart a day, counting what he had at bars on the way home.

Did he often not show up for work? Naw, maybe once in a while when he was sick. How often? Maybe once every couple of weeks. How many times the previous month? Well, that was a bad month. He missed eleven out of twenty-two working days, but it was the flu season. Had he gone to a doctor? No, no reason to go; it was just the flu. Had his wife covered for him by telephoning the plant? Yeah. He felt too rotten to talk to anyone. Did he go anywhere on those days? Oh, a couple of times he went to the corner saloon to play the pinball machines.

Did the company single him out or were others given the same attention? Hell, the company does it all the time. How did they do it? His supervisor had a talk with him after work in the steel plant yard, told him the company wanted him to see a company counselor. Did his supervisor say he was drinking too much? No, he just said his work was slipping and he thought the counselor might help him figure out why. Next, the counselor asked a lot of questions including some about drinking, then referred him to a plant doctor specializing in alcoholism and it was the doctor who said he had a boozing problem that would soon be out of control, if it wasn't already, and told him he would have to get treatment or be disciplined, even fired.

A union representative was present at both these latter meetings, but said little until they were over. Then he told the worker that the union endorsed and participated in the system; the union considered the doctor's recommendation the best course for the union, the company, and especially for the worker himself; the worker's reaction was "that pious son-of-a-bitch."

This is a bare-bones outline of how things went; altogether, it took several hours of formal therapy and informal discussion. After a predictable two-week period, the steelworker began to sense there was something wrong with his story. It just didn't hang together.

Most of the discussions centered on the man's job. But the personal side, the family side, was more dramatic. The man himself told us subsequently that his wife had been a mess. She felt she didn't have the money or time to get professional help for him, for the children or for herself. He became a slob around the house and while there was no physical abuse, the children either were ignored or yelled at. The two boys began getting into serious teen-age jams and the girl took out her anxieties in eating and was alarmingly obese at the age of 13. The wife, on the other hand, ate little, was sick much of the time and became a loose sack of bones. Thus something with the imposing and impersonal name of Labor-Management Committee on Occupational Alcoholism saved not only a job, but a family.

It's a Walt Disney ending, but the last I heard, my friend was doing well, was back at work, had been pro-moted and had a home life more pleasant than he had considered possible.

The labor-management programs are basically sim-ple. In any business establishment they involve everyone in management, from the chairman of the board down to the most humble straw boss. To be successful, they must include unions on an equal basis. Industry has a legitimate right to expect satisfactory performances by its employees; labor has a legitimate right to protect its members from unfair or discriminatory practices.

To start, top company officials and labor represent-atives get together and set up a committee. That sounds like the end of the whole idea. But this is a working committee, or should be. Its creation is a beginning. The committee draws up a program, guidelines for which are available from several sources, including the National Council on Alcoholism, which pioneered the field.

A good program would start by educating both man-agement and employees on such basics as the fact that alcoholism is nothing to be ashamed of, but a disease with no social stigma; social drinking is of no concern to the company or the union; the program is interested only in the effect of alcoholism on the employees' work; coopera-tion with the program will help the employees' careers, not damage them; if they reject attempts to bring them out of their drinking they will be disciplined, with dismissal the last resort.

The bosses—everyone with supervisory authority—must be taught to appraise only an employee's job performance, not his personal habits. If his efficiency goes down, no supervisor must conclude it is due to drinking; few supervisors are qualified to judge. Instead the employee must be persuaded to see a specially trained counselor or doctor who will go into the question of why the slump. It may be due to other physical or mental malfunctions; it may be due to excessive debt or a lousy home life or any one of dozens of circumstances.

The counselor channels the employee to experts on whatever he thinks is wrong—for our purposes, alcoholism. If the counselor's diagnosis is deemed correct, the employee is urged to get treatment, sometimes through monitored attendance at meetings of Alcoholics Anonymous, sometimes at rehabilitation centers, sometimes through out-patient therapy.

All of this should be completely confidential. And it should be done without humiliating the employee, whether he be a company vice president, a union executive, or just a rank-and-file laborer. He should be treated as would anybody else with a major disease.

Obviously, such programs can be abused if improperly run. A supervisor who dislikes an employee can pass the word upstairs that so-and-so is a drunk and should be fired. One man I knew, who drank very little, claims this happened to him because the boss's wife had the hots for him. A woman acquaintance contended she was turned in as an alcoholic because she was thought to be trying to get her supervisor's job. The truth was she was not a drunk and she planned to retire to raise a family; the supervisor was tinged with paranoia and was subsequently himself given psychiatric attention.

These are all reasons for providing that employees can have union representatives with them at all consultations. Unless an employee is extraordinarily unpopular, the union usually will protect him. But if the employee is indeed an alcoholic, an honorable union normally wants a reformation as much as does the company. After all, an incompetent worker can give an entire unit a poor performance rating and can even physically endanger others, as in a steel plant.

The company holds the ace, particularly when it has union agreement. It can fire the alcoholic. Unless the employee is destined for a skid row dump, that's a very potent argument for doing what he's told.

Most of what we have gone into here deals with outright alcoholics, but the labor-management programs have a more subtle aspect. The debilitating affects of alcohol very often first show up in a person's work. There are a number of possible reasons but the fact is that shrewd observation of work performance can sometimes spot alcoholism in its earliest stages, when it might normally be classified merely as "hard" social drinking. Exactly where one ends and the other begins is extremely difficult to delineate. The separation might be where the drinking becomes sufficiently heavy to affect work patterns. It would seem axiomatic that the earlier alcoholism is detected, the easier it is to treat. In view of the exertion required to "cure" an alcoholic, almost any effort to prevent a heavy drinker from becoming an alcoholic must be considered worthwhile. To be preppy about it, an ounce of prevention is worth a pound of cure—or care.

Thus, as what might be called a semi-preventive device, the labor-management programs, though financed through health and medical insurance, save money by avoiding possibly overwhelming medical costs as the disease progresses. Many health programs do not cover treatment for alcoholism as such, but a sizable percentage of their subscribers get treatment nonetheless under different labels. Their doctors or they themselves may camouflage their illnesses as the usual cirrhosis, or heart failure or something—even psychiatric difficulties. In one way, this is helpful because it circumvents the tag of alcoholism, resented and rejected by so many. But it runs up the cost. Treatment for symptomatic diseases resulting from alcoholism often requires in-patient hospital care, which is usually far more expensive than an alcoholic rehabilitation center.

Sympathy, common sense, and statistics dictate that a labor-management plan include and actively involve the families of employees concerned. The family of an alcoholic, or an incipient alcoholic, has suffered along with the drinker and the company. As an example of how the family shares the misery, the National Council on Alcoholism tells of one study made on a group of thirty men and women who did not themselves drink but had drinking problems in their immediate families. The results were compared with those coming from another carefully matched control group of non-drinkers with no family alcoholic problems. The comparison showed that sick leave for the non-tainted control group cost a total of $3,105.60 for one year. For the non-drinkers with family drinking problems, the cost was $34,487.72 for the same one-year period, more than ten times as much.

The non-drinkers with booze problems around them found the family problems time-consuming distractions that cost them and the company money.

There are other studies that produced similar results, bearing out with figures the much-used statement that alcoholism is not an individual problem but a family problem.

In addition to the discomfort and all-around torment a

drinker can create, families should for other reasons welcome efforts such as those of the labor-management committees. The company and the union take over the uproar and bitterness and have experts to handle them. The family does not accuse the employee of excessive drinking; people with knowledge and authority do that. The responsibility for picking a place of treatment and for persuading the employee to go are assigned to somebody else. So is the cost. No more nasty confrontations, no more long-lasting resentments that might otherwise permanently wreck a family even if the alcoholic is successfully put back together. Perhaps most important, the often unpleasant task of getting a person into treatment will be taken over by people who have the biggest club—the threat of job dismissal, with its attendant possibilities of extreme financial suffering, blacklisting, loss of union benefits and numerous others.

Any group of family or friends that has ever tried to rescue an alcoholic, or a potential alcoholic, would be delighted to have someone else take care of it. And in those cases of which I have direct knowledge, help from the boss is sought when appropriate and it can be decisive. It is characteristic of many alcoholics that their jobs are more important than their families. The alcoholic often knows, however much he may deny he is an alcoholic, that his family is aware of his condition. Even though his working conditions may be unpleasant, he thinks of his job as a sanctuary, removed from the critical atmosphere of home. And most important unless he is in an advanced stage of alcoholism, he will realize that without a job he could not finance his drinking.

But even if the company and union do a good share of the dirty work, the family still has an essential part in the proceedings. If it has the will and the courage to do so, it can provide support for the drinker while he is a patient. He should not be coddled, but it can help his recovery if he feels he is not totally alone. On this point we can find a wide range of opinion, but I personally do not think I would have made it without the support of my two daughters. I am sure neither thought I would make it; they had good reasons for being dubious. When I was kicked out of the last rehabilitation center, they deserted me, properly figuring that I probably had not been successful, but if I had I must go the rest of the way on my own. That was the best decision they could have made. But their assistance while I was still a patient was helpful. Our relations now, incidentally, are excellent.

Normally, the family also has an important function after the patient leaves the rehabilitation center—during the period of "aftercare" that I have already talked about. The patient himself is responsible for much of his own aftercare, through AA, his own firmness, counseling if needed, and other devices. But the amount of good or harm the family behavior can do is incalculable.

Supporters of the labor-management idea claim it has a high success rate; I have seen figures of from 65 percent to 85 percent, and they are more plausible than some other estimates because, presumably, an employee who accepts and responds to treatment continues to work for the company, hence can be assessed for a longer period. The people in Alcoholics Anonymous and most of those in rehabilitation centers are so transient that it is difficult to keep track of them for any length of time.

Also, the labor-management groups are better equipped to appraise the virtues and weaknesses of the various rehab facilities available so the chances are lessened of a patient winding up in a bummer. And most of the patients, highly motivated by the threat of joblessness, have little inclination to goof off. They know the results of not getting and not responding to treatment will be far worse than the treatment—negative motivation with positive results.

Selection of rehabilitation institutions of high quality has a tangential benefit: it should or could raise the general quality level in an area that is otherwise regulated little. A few states have high standards and enforce them, but not many. The care with which treatment centers are picked by labor-management programs is understandable since the company, the union and the insurance holders want returns on their money. They want the employees once again to do the best work they can.

The choosing of higher quality rehabilitation places may be responsible for the fact that any worker who responds to treatment, no matter how startled and angry he is when he is fingered, feels good about the company when it's over. He considers paternalism fine when it helps him.

The biggest drawback of the labor-management program may be its relatively slow growth. Many larger companies have adopted the system, have even advertised it. Others have gone through the motions but have not pushed it to its full potential. Some have, in practice, limited it to the lower-ranking employees and in effect exempted top executives where a botched-up mind can do the most damage. Or, on occasion, it has worked the other way around.

A factor in the relatively slow growth of the programs is their initial cost; many ledger-minded administrators are unable to appreciate anything beyond tomorrow's income-and-outgo figures. Another factor is an inability to comprehend how damaging and costly alcoholism can be. One fairly high company official told me he couldn't see why the stockholders should pay to "sober somebody up." "We'll just fire him," he said," there are plenty of people who would like his job." What had not penetrated his walled-in mind was that the company had considerable money invested in its personnel. In one company, of the people I knew who were canned for poor work resulting from drinking, three of them had a total of almost ninety years' experience. The company had spent hundreds of thousands of dollars giving them that training. Three new men had to be given the same ninety years' instruction and background before they could approach the theoretical skills of the men they replaced.

Still another factor is the reluctance of some company directors to admit that some of their employees drink excessively. They consider it a blot on their own escutcheons. The standard reaction is "why our people wouldn't do that!" The shocked executive himself may just have returned from a nineteenth-hole celebration at the local country club.

So the alcohol-control programs are not unanimously popular. But what hard facts are available indicate alcoholism, or excessive drinking, costs the country's economy huge amounts of money; the labor-management programs are worthy from a humanitarian standpoint, in the best sense of the word. Organized labor has supported the program, from AFL-CIO headquarters down—and sideways. Properly run, the programs can prevent alcoholism as well as "cure" it, and have many beneficial side-effects, the most inspiring of which is the saving of souls from degradation, despair, and death.

10

Doctors in Alcoholism

Doctors are getting the word. They are being told alcoholism is a disease, that it is treatable; they are being told how it should be treated, clinically and psychologically; they are being told they should be important parts of the treatment, which collectively they now are not. The trouble is, judging from past performances, too few are listening.

Who is doing the telling? No less an organization than the American Medical Association, or at least an enlightened, sympathetic element of the AMA. Alcoholism has been recognized by the AMA as an illness since 1956. The AMA was not first; the World Health Organization took the same action five years earlier and even before that—in 1943 and 1944 two private companies—DuPont and Eastman Kodak had in effect classified alcoholism as an ailment, not a habit. Yet thousands upon thousands of individual doctors have been dragging their intellectual and professional feet. In the words of a 1977 AMA publication, "they have been unduly slow in recognizing alcoholism as an illness and, in practice, have tended to dismiss alcoholics as hopeless or, at best, unpleasant and unrewarding patients."

Those words are taken from perhaps the most surprising and in many ways most satisfying document I have read on alcoholism. It has the simple title *Manual on Alcoholism*, copyrighted and published by the American Medical Association. It is actually a primer for doctors. But aside from relatively short passages on the clinical aspects of the disease—laden with medical terms such as "telangiectasias," "gynecomastia," and "epistaxis"—it is clear, sensible, and understandable even to a thick-headed, English-speaking layman such as I.

One of the intriguing and perhaps frightening aspects of the book is its simplicity. It begins at the beginning and in words of two syllables explains what alcoholism is all about, from its economic effects to its ultimate treatment. Years ago, I was flabbergasted at my own ignorance of the problem, and the ignorance of my friends and relatives; I am even more astonished that a good many doctors, after umpteen years of schooling and training, apparently know little more than did I. The booklet might be a text for a high school course. And it is magnificently done.

Much of what it says I have gone into previously in this book, in different ways and with different emphasis, but with few if any basic disagreements. The book's introduction cites the recent changes in public attitudes toward alcoholism; "previously," it says, "we were essentially judgmental and moralistic . . . Expressions of open disapproval, condemnation and rejection were common." Now the public is more inclined to help.

The medical profession, says the book, also is changing, due to "the physician's own increased recognition of his obligations to a neglected group of patients, and his determination to meet and fulfill his responsibilities." The AMA is correct and smart to put the matter in positive language, because expressed negatively, it means the physician has not fully realized his obligation to a neglected group of patients and has not tried strenuously to fulfill his responsibilities.

The book stresses the scope of the problem, including alcoholism among women and young people. It cites well-worn but perhaps inexact figures such as estimates that alcohol is involved in some fashion with 64 percent of all homicides, 41 percent of assaults, 34 percent of rapes, 30 percent of suicides, 60 percent of child abuse, 50 percent of automobile accidents fatal to drivers, and 33 percent of those fatal to adult pedestrians.

Here is a summary of some of the points made by the AMA manual:

In spite of contrary views, alcoholism most logically can be classified as a *highly complex illness*.

While there are "literally hundreds" of definitions of alcoholism, the greatest measure of agreement seems to come on this: "Alcoholism is an illness characterized by significant impairment that is directly associated with persistent and excessive use of alcohol. Impairment may involve physiological, psychological or social disfunction." Put more basically but probably less precisely, when your drinking damages your health, mind, or the everyday functions of living, such as work or home life, you can be categorized as an alcoholic.

There is no one cause of alcoholism, but rather a complicated mixture of physical, mental, and social factors. Alcohol by itself is not the cause, any more than marriage is the cause of divorce or sugar the cause of diabetes. Most of those who drink do not become alcoholics. There seems to be no such thing as an "alcoholic personality," and genetic factors—the inheritance of alcoholic tendencies—have not been established conclusively.

Alcohol messes up the central nervous system and is a

depressant whose discomforts can be eased quickly and temporarily by another drink—which may contribute to an addiction to alcohol but which does not cause it.

Uncertainty about causes of alcoholism may be a major reason doctors are reluctant to tackle it. How does a physician treat something when he doesn't know what it is or what brought it on? The uncertainties extend to the psychological and sociological areas as well as the physiological.

WHAT THE BODY DOES WITH ALCOHOL

Getting more deeply into the medical aspects of alcohol, and what it does in and to the body, the manual makes the point that alcohol is absorbed more rapidly through the small intestine than through the stomach. Enough soaks through from the stomach to give the "quick jolt" effect so prized by heavy drinkers, but the relatively slow development of true inebriation comes after the alcohol makes its way into the small intestine. The general belief, I believe, even among the most experienced drinkers, has been that the damage (or good) is done in the stomach and that shielding the stomach with food will diminish or eliminate the drunkenness. Eating while drinking will slow down the inebriation process because the food delays passage of the alcohol into the small intestine. But it is more a matter of time than severity.

The manual goes into the problems of differentiating between an alcoholic and a heavy social drinker or an alcohol abuser. Most of these I have already laid out as best I can, but the AMA's summary of guidelines is very much to the point. Translating them into my own words, the book says alcoholism should be suspected if the patient has a history of:

- Steadily increasing drinking, whether it is sporadic or constant;

- Drinking when faced with psychological or physical problems, to lessen the distress;
- Thinking mostly about having a drink and the need of a drink;
- Sneaking or gulping drinks just for the effect and not for reasons of sociability;
- Making alibis and excuses for drinking;
- Refusing to admit to drinking too much and getting irritated when such a suggestion is made;
- Being absent from work too often;
- Switching jobs frequently, often to lesser assignments, and winding up in a spot below the worker's capabilities;
- Looking shabbier and dirtier than he has any good reason to;
- Complaining persistently about his health—insomnia, stomachaches, headaches and loss of appetite;
- Making frequent trips to the doctor for distress that stems from booze;
- Having chronic marital and family problems;
- Having a record of arrests, particularly for drunkenness or drunken driving.

These are conditions the doctor legitimately can look for; he may have to consult with families and friends to get the facts—always, of course, with the patient's permission. If he finds several of the characteristic circumstances, he probably is heading in the right direction. The AMA's guidelines constitute an excellent basis for judgment, but there are, as previously detailed, many more signs, such as incoherent conversation, scrambled reasoning, muscular clumsiness, lack of concentration, and forgetfulness.

On the physical side, the manual points out there are few obvious indications of alcoholism in the early stages of the disease. But as it progresses, more clues appear, such as hand tremors—the shakes. Then there is the red face and bulbous W. C. Fields nose—acne rosacea—and bruises in unusual places. In the southern part of the country, a rash of serious fire ant stings over the body may mean the patient has passed out, or tried to sleep it off, in the weeds; a parallel condition in northern states is frostbite.

Then there are spider angiomas of the chest, more commonly known simply as "spiders." They are the webs of dilated blood vessels that aren't quite big enough to qualify as varicose veins but are nevertheless noticeable. And ugly. More uncomfortable is disseminated nummular eczema, which manifests itself as dry blotches of skin that itch and often damage the appetites of bystanders. Of course, far more serious indications of alcoholism show up with time.

When it gets around to treatment for alcoholism, the AMA manual concedes the matter is too complicated to be handled comprehensively in a booklet that is intended as a basic guide for doctors. If simplified too much, it might have become a series of formulas that limit treatment and fast become outdated. So the book attempts a compromise, and for my money, succeeds. It outlines some of the conditions under which a patient should be admitted to a general hospital and/or to a psychiatric hospital, and how he should be handled in the institution. The manual, incidentally, repeatedly emphasizes a point too often overlooked: anyone admitted to treatment for alcoholism should be examined carefully for injuries such as skull fracture, concussion, torn ligaments, and a raft of others. A drunk has a habit of falling down, or bumping into things, and in his anesthetized state can do serious damage to himself and not feel a thing. The alcohol also can conceal the damage in the hospital; not all comas are alcohol-induced. The manual also stresses that sedatives, so freely passed out by some physicians, must be administered with great care; the drunken patient is already sedated, perhaps dangerously so.

So the manual goes, through almost all the known aspects of alcoholism, from recognition to aftercare management. While it is written for doctors, its wisdom is not buried in verbiage, nor for the most part, in that strange language used by men of medicine. As a sample of what I consider the manual's grasp of the subject, the depth and breadth of its understanding, I was given permission to quote from one portion which appears in the manual under the heading "Psychiatric Treatment and Long Range Rehabilitation." The quoted passage is self-illuminating:

"Vital and often life-saving as the acute management of the alcoholic may be, it is the long haul of rehabilitation that is the test of therapeutic effectiveness. Very few disorders, and especially alcoholism, lend themselves to a simple and one-sided approach. Certainly in the rehabilitation process we have to consider the usefulness of the physician as counselor, of formal psychotherapy, and of medications, socializations and life-support programs.

"It is not at all unusual for physicians to express a lack of confidence in their ability to treat patients whose illnesses have strong emotional components, as is commonly the case with alcoholics. Concern over saying or doing the wrong thing, and thus causing harm instead of helping, frequently is based on a mistaken belief that successful treatment demands thorough knowledge and mastery of psychiatric principles and techniques. This insecurity can lead to denial of interest in such patients and their problems, with resulting indifference, outright rejection, or perhaps rapid referral to a colleague. A lack of confidence is unfortunate from many standpoints, particularly because it is seldom justified and rarely benefits anyone, least of all the patient.

"More serious and complicated cases, of course, should be referred to a specialist after adequate evaluation, and consultation should be sought whenever there is doubt or as soon as the need for such help becomes apparent.

"It may reassure the physician to recall that there are emotional components to every illness, components he has learned to deal with through his own individual techniques. Most of the skills required in his management of patients whose emotional problems predominate are not only familiar to him but have become integral to his manner and approach. To be effective with such cases, he must learn to emphasize these skills and to be fully aware he is doing so, but it is not necessary for him to learn new or seemingly unfathomable methods of treatment. There simply is no substitute for genuine interest in the patient as a person, concern over his welfare, and earnest desire to help him in whatever ways are necessary, all of which are quickly perceived and usually responded to favorably.

"No simple approach utilizing specific interview techniques can be recommended as the only one to employ in communicating with the alcoholic patient. That which is most natural to the physician and simultaneously most helpful to the patient is the one to seek. It perhaps goes without saying that consideration of the patient's dignity as a human being is essential to any therapeutic relationship, regardless of circumstances. In addition, unusual patience with the alcoholic often is required, particularly at the outset. Moving too rapidly sometimes proves so threatening either to the patient or to the physician that a new beginning is required.

"The patient with alcoholism usually is highly sensitive about his condition, often denying the existence of the illness both to himself and to others. He may not really intend to be deceitful. Rather he frequently rationalizes his drinking habits in a vigorous effort to convince all concerned (including himself) that there are no problems associated with his use of alcohol. The fact that he is an alcoholic can be so frightening and depressing to him that he may well be incapable of admitting it. Also, if he is consciously aware of being an alcoholic, he probably expects hostile rejection and disapproval, whenever the matter is discussed, from those whose support he needs the most.

"It is not unusual for the alcoholic patient to be brought to the physician under duress, forced by his own or, more likely, another's desperation. Feelings of guilt, embarrassment and depression in such a humiliating situation are not at all remarkable. One can understand and even appreciate the urgency the alcoholic is likely to feel in his desire to retreat at the earliest possible opportunity. Emphatic denial of any problems whatever will probably seem to him the most expedient way to escape, even though he may at the same time wish to be helped.

"Finally, physical and psychological dependence upon alcohol can be so intense that the patient is unable to think much beyond returning to his supply. The prospect of facing the future without alcohol produces such anxiety and panic that he may feel obligated to resort to trickery, deception, cajolery or whatever facilitates the resumption of drinking.

"It is readily apparent that under any of these circumstances, bold or direct confrontation may well prove extremely disturbing to the alcoholic. Harshness and abruptness in manner are alienating forces in any physician-patient relationship, and perhaps particularly so in this kind of situation. If the physician has a *callous* attitude, it will in all probability destroy his rapport permanently.

"This is not to say the physician should not be *matter-of-fact* in his approach. Often this is necessary to face and deal with specific issues. There is little other choice, for example, when the patient's health and welfare are so seriously jeopardized that prompt action is required. Indeed, obvious demonstration of awareness of the patient's condition, an honest concern for his well-being, and an expressed intention of helping him are needed if treatment is to progress. Such demonstration, however, does not require the abandonment of understanding, tact, patience and discretion. A reasonable investment of time to provide them generally will pay ample dividends.

"*Excessive 'understanding' intended to maintain a pleasant relationship nullifies effectiveness.* An overly-tolerant attitude on the part of the physician may create an aura of cordiality between the physician and the alcoholic, but it does little to help the patient face the realities of his situation or to assume appropriate responsiblity for helping himself. Patronizing seldom disguises underlying hostility, and whether intentional or not, it is perceived quickly as being a false representation of feelings. The patient may regard it as a weakness or lack of interest and ability on the part of the physician, either of which can destroy his confidence and make the physician's efforts ineffective. In turn, the patient may express his own hostility by appearing overly compliant or defiantly uncooperative. The net gain in either case can be negligible at best.

"A firm, consistent, accepting and reasonable attitude toward the patient and his illness proves superior and is more likely to make the treatment program successful.

"*The patient's word should be accepted whenever possible.* One must recognize again that denial is most often the alcoholic's major defense. On the other hand, the patient may admit glibly to having a problem with alcohol, hoping that the matter will not be pursued farther. In either situation, it is difficult to obtain reliable or adequate factual information from him.

"In contrast to the dearth of background material which may be gained from the patient, an abundance can be derived from other sources. The spouse, a relative, a friend, a business associate, or any number of other persons frequently volunteer seemingly endless details about the patient's drinking habits, behavior and problems. Quite commonly, the physician finds their reports desirable or even required for his proper orientation and perspective. The reliability of *all* information, whether from the patient or others, must be weighed carefully before any of it is acceptable as fact.

"It is *not* appropriate for the physician to seek accounts from others without the patients' *expressed consent.* The request for authorization to make inquiry may lead the patient himself to give a more comprehensive history. But unless the reasons behind the request are explained, it may succeed only in alienating the patient and making him even more defensive.

"Evidence which contradicts his statements should be presented to him quite frankly, and general themes of reports from others need to be discussed with him, although it is seldom necessary to go into minute detail. Whenever he is able to do so, the physician should accept the patient's version as factual. In situations of conflict, as between husbands and wives, objectivity is extremely important, and care is necessary to avoid taking sides on issues or serving as a referee. The patient, however, usually has a genuine need to believe that the physician has confidence and trust in him.

"*Physicians should make clinical, not moral, judgments.* It may seem an affront to a physician to suggest that he guard against moralism when dealing with alcoholic patients. Yet possible resentment hopefully will be tempered by the observation that moralism is hardly a fault when properly applied.

"The physician is expected to be a moral person, to have high ideals, integrity, responsibility, and a sense of right and wrong. Courage and strength are necessary for handling difficult situations. It cannot really seem extraordinary, despite deeply indoctrinated strains of objectivity, that his own moral standards may at times become entwined in the mechanics of his clinical judgment.

"Every person experiences frustrations and disappointments throughout his lifetime. It is a requirement of maturity to learn to deal with them effectively and to postpone immediate pleasures for more enduring and more substantial ones at a later time. Everyone, however, retains elements of immaturity, such as the *desire* for dependence and for prompt gratification of wishes. In the more mature individual, these elements are recognized or demonstrated only in extreme circumstances. A person sometimes is made aware of them in himself, either consciously or unconsciously, when he sees such characteristics blatantly displayed by another. It is understandable, then, that immaturity as shown by an alcoholic can prove offensive to others (including physicians) and anger them. This may be due to the fact that it is disconcerting to be reminded of one's own immature side, or it may be a result in part of unrecognized envy that the alcoholic seemingly can "get away with it," while the observer cannot.

"The physician needs to be acutely aware of his own feelings if he is to prevent them from exerting inappropriate influence upon his relationships with patients or their families.

"Finally, it must be pointed out that in all probability there will be times when a stern manner is both indicated and justified. It can even be a determining factor in establishing limitations of acceptable behavior on the part of the patient or perhaps of family members. Introspection will establish whether the reaction is appropriate, or more a reflection of unrecognized anger and negativism, and therefore moralistic. The ability to distinguish moral judgment from clinical judgment, to recognize their proper balance and application, is, after all, part of the total wisdom the physician seeks to achieve.

   "'Success' and 'failure' in reaching the alcoholic patient should not be taken at face value. Successful management of his patients' illnesses is rightfully of primary concern and importance to the physician. It may also be vital to the physician's self-image and self-confidence, a factor which can contribute to unsuspected reluctance to accept patients with presumably poor prognoses or those with illnesses having an unfortunate stigma. Most patients have an instinctive awareness of this consideration, and their consequent desire to please the physician can be a useful motivating force in their recovery. On the other hand, this awareness partially explains why some seriously ill persons delay seeking medical attention even when they are very much aware intellectually that they should have it.

   "Recalling the psychodynamics of alcoholism can aid in understanding why the alcoholic patient may try to please or, at other times, may openly antagonize the physician. The patient's past experiences of being or feeling rejected by others lead him to expect the same reaction sooner or later from the physician, even though he may be aware that the physician recognizes his need for protection and help. If compliance is used by the patient to forestall rejection and achieve comfort, either or both parties may become elated and over-confident with this evidence of apparent success, which in reality may be illusory. This can, in fact, seriously interfere with progress. Lack of cooperation or defiance, on the other hand, is sometimes the patient's way of testing the physician's interest or of 'proving' that no one can help him. Ironically, this very attitude may prove to be a key to his eventual improvement.

"Successes, especially early ones, should therefore be viewed with guarded optimism. Apparent failures, on the other hand, certainly should not be considered reflections upon the physician's ability nor barriers to his further effort.

"An understanding of the nature of this therapeutic relationship gives a good foundation to whatever special rehabilitative techniques may be applied. Understanding is essential if psychotherapeutic techniques are indicated.

"The definition of the goals of treatment and the obstacles to their attainment will assist in determining which type of rehabilitative program should be recommended. Certainly, most would agree eventual and indefinite abstinence has the highest priority.

"In 1974, the AMA Committee on Alcoholism issued a statement jointly with the National Council on Alcoholism regarding the role of abstinence in recovery from alcoholism. Nothing in the intervening years has invalidated any of the following four points made in that statement:

"1. Abstinence from alcohol is necessary for recovery from the disease of alcoholism.

"2. Although abstinence is a means of achieving recovery, other factors by which a person's life are enriched are important: improved physical and emotional health, better work performance, more rewarding relationships with the family and society and increased economic efficiency.

"3. As in many other diseases, relapses may take

place but must never be thought to indicate that recovery is beyond reach. Any improvement is positive and should be recognized and encouraged as a prelude to recovery.

"4. There is need for responsible research into alternative approaches, carried out with proper controls as well as the judicious publication of results when pertinent.

"At this time we do not have sufficient evidence to confirm that controlled drinking is a possibility for a diagnosed alcoholic, although some studies have suggested it.

"While abstinence is easily accomplished in the hospital, how can we best achieve this for the long course? Beyond abstinence, what other physical, mental, marital and social problems does the patient experience?

"In the broadest sense, treatment of the alcoholic patient is directed toward helping him find a new way of life. A variety of treatment modalities can be useful in achieving this, including individual and group psychotherapy, 'counseling' of several kinds, psychotropic medication, and more specialized techniques such as family therapy and behavior modification. The type or types of therapy undertaken by the physician should be determined by the individual patient's needs and community resources and be in accordance with the physician's interests and skills.

"Whatever specific methods are employed, psychiatric treatment should provide the patient with the emotional support of sympathetic understanding, acceptance, and encouragement, so that his sense of functional adequacy may be enhanced. Treatment should give him very practical support, especially early in the program, when the patient needs the kind of assistance that is reality focused and genuinely helpful to his endeavors to solve the immediate problems he faces.

"Ultimately, treatment should bring about a general reorientation that will equip the patient to deal with, and adjust to, everyday pressures inherent in living, without the need to drink. The goal is to make the patient realize that his life can be more rewarding without the use of alcohol than with it, and to help him find substitutive emotional satisfaction. Discussions directed at finding out why he believes he should, can or must drink as he does can help the patient discover ways to manage without alcohol.

"The physician must start from the basic point where the alcoholic is struggling, and deal with immediate problems first. He must approach them with an objective view toward the patient's own attitudes and feelings about his problems and how they are affecting him. For example, even though many patients will have found that their present situations have become impossible and unbearable, it is difficult for them to accept the fact they are alcoholics and must do without alcohol. One of the most significant aspects of the physician's effectiveness at the beginning often involves helping them to accept the truth. It is also important to help the patient understand clearly from the start that whatever he does to improve, he does for himself and not for someone else, such as his spouse or a family member. He needs guidance first in learning something about what his true attitudes and feelings actually are, and then in appreciating how and why they developed and why they have led him into alcoholism.

"Treatment should be goal oriented, with immediate as well as more long-range objectives in mind, and with new goals delineated as earlier ones are achieved. The goals set by the physician should be realistic for the individual patient and consistent with his potential. Stereotyped regimens should be avoided; the physician must be willing to modify both goals and methods in accordance with current and changing circumstances."

✳ ✳ ✳ ✳ ✳

So it goes, this astonishing manual, for 100 pages. On the final page, it says total abstinence is vitally necessary for some people and desirable for many others; but trying to eliminate the use of alcohol entirely for the whole population would not only be unpopular but probably impossible. We tried it once in this country, and I am convinced that the glamor and thrilling illegality of drinking during Prohibition gave a tremendous boost to the consumption of alcohol.

The booklet ends on what may strike some as a strange note but which actually is earthy and practical. "Unfortunately, but not surprisingly," it says, "the physician and his family are not immune to alcoholism. . . . They may require a concerned and caring colleague to intervene." In honest fact, doctors may be among the more vulnerable people, so far as alcoholism is concerned. And where other drugs are concerned, physicians are not only exposed to them but they are in a sense immersed in them. So it is that organized physicians in a number of states have put together groups to help their colleagues who become entrapped. My understanding is that the help-groups, whatever they are called formally, have done a brisk business from their inception, which is good news for the rest of us.

But the most significant thrust of the *Manual on Alcoholism* is that it demonstrates the American Medical Association is moving on what it describes as "a genuine public health problem in every section of this country." The movement began some time ago, but now has begun to reach impressive power. At the beginning of this book, I pointed out that anyone confronted with an alcohol problem thinks first of a doctor, but too often the physician is useless.

That is an accurate generalization, but it won't be for long if the manual is widely enough read. The AMA, half in fun, calls it a bestseller—which is not intended to put it in a class with *Gone With the Wind*. The book is in demand from the people it is intended to reach and who we should all hope it will reach. It is now in its third printing and another revision and another printing is in preparation as this is written, which indicates a growing recognition even among doctors that alcoholism is a ghastly problem that has not always been forcefully and intelligently attacked.

Medical opposition to heavier emphasis on alcoholism is not necessarily frivolous nor the result of ignorance. A great many physicians still do not consider it a specific illness and treatable as an entity. And a good number are opposed to any avoidable additional fragmentation of medicine, either in medical schools or in practices. Only recently has emergency medicine been recognized as a specialty. But now so much of medicine is specialized that the old-fashioned general practitioner may be an endangered species.

The very fact that the *Manual on Alcoholism* is getting considerable circulation in the medical profession is an indication of how little the members of the profession know about an ailment that hits perhaps one out of ten of us. Very little in the book was new to me—a layman. Doctors, like so many of us, do get set in their ways and their slowness to appreciate the gravity of the alcoholism plague is understandable. But it has slowed research and left a cavernous hole in the potential treatment of alcoholics. It has stimulated a tremendous growth of rehabilitation clinics, for which we should be thankful; but along with the good ones have come institutions more interested in making money than in saving the sick. The doctor, the person who most logically should handle the situation, has been skipped over.

If enough physicians read and profit from the AMA

manual, the enormous gap in the treatment of alcoholics will start to be filled. It may involve more than a mere awareness of alcoholism as a disease; it may require a change in attitudes. I have had doctors sneer at me for praising rehabilitation clinics. If a drunk doesn't know or doesn't care that he is killing himself, they ask me, who can help him? The effective rehab establishment can help, that's who. But a high proportion of doctors with whom I have talked don't know what alcoholic-care units do, or how they do it.

11

Rehabilitating for Money

The care and treatment of alcoholics is, has been, will be, and should be a profitable business. Judging from the increase in recent years in the number of rehabilitation centers, it may be on its way to becoming Big Business.

When I was a child, an institution devoted to the care of drunks was regarded with a mixture of ridicule, horror, and bafflement. Ridicule, because anything about a drunk was somehow considered ridiculous, perhaps because of the tendency to ridicule what you don't understand. Horror, because the inmates were seldom seen in public; the institution's grounds, though often well kept, seemed forbidding and were definitely off limits to the public. And bafflement because practically no outsiders knew what went on inside the places nor what sort of horrible monsters were locked within.

Such, at least, is my recollection. I can remember taking frequent family drives in our Model T touring car past a lovely old Maryland mansion with great rolling sweeps of lawn and immaculate evergreen plantings. But it was somehow sinister. Never did I see anyone, even a caretaker, outside. Nor was there ever a car in the driveway nor a raised curtain. I asked my grandmother, my uncle, my mother what it was, since it struck me as a bit of grim and mysterious elegance that I desperately wanted to know more about.

The only answers I got were "sh's" or "it's sort of a hospital," or "it's a home for kind of crazy people." Not until I tackled my older brother, sophisticated and experienced far beyond his calendar age, was I told it was a home for drunks. Obviously, if that's what it was, the drunks or their families had money, and the family's idea of treating a drunk was to keep him concealed, as with any other scandal.

Today, however, if a drunk can make his fingers stagger through the Yellow Pages, he can actually find advertisements for those once-shameful places. Sometimes the columns of advertisements are delightfully brutal in their pitch. "Has Your Life Been Ruined by Drinking?" or "If You Are a Drunk, We Can Help!"

And there are television commercials, with similar wording and explicit messages. Alcoholism and its treatment is discussed in schools, at club meetings, on the lecture circuits, even in bars.

This does not mean there has been a tremendous increase in alcoholism, but rather in public awareness of the illness and of the need for treatment. There can be an argument over which came first—the awareness or the publicity. Whichever the origin, the change seems to fit the trend to face once-unmentionable problems openly—from feminine hygiene to venereal disease. And it is a welcome transformation from the days when an institution for alcoholics was mentioned in the same ominous whispers that older people reserved for the "poorhouse," or the "lunatic asylum."

Chains of rehabilitation centers have developed, with

typical corporate structures; not only do they advertise their product, but they have trade associations and they sell stock, issue financial reports, and otherwise behave as business enterprises. As I said before, I can see nothing intrinsically wrong with this. Almost everything else in the country theoretically is operated for profit—that's our system. Doctors, dentists, nurses, X-ray laboratories, hospitals, nursing homes—almost everything has to make money or it shuts down.

Some of my purist friends deplore the presence of the profit motive in the alcoholism area; no one, they say, should make money out of forlorn drunks. Alcoholics Anonymous, they point out, is almost totally untainted by money. All that is fine. It is noble thinking, I guess, but I would rather see somebody make a few bucks in saving an alcoholic, than have the alcoholic obliterated by the bottle. The thousands of dollars that I spent, and that were spent on me, were—for me—the best investment that could have been made.

Incidentally, the growth of alcoholism centers has in some cases been a boon to hospitals operating on close margins. They have converted empty bed space into revenue-producing rehabilitation units.

The National Association of Alcoholism Treatment Programs (NAATP) is a trade association. At the time I talked with its Executive Director, Michael Q. Ford, its headquarters were in Irvine, California, which seemed the center of the alcohol-treatment activity and growth. The NAATP's goals are those of similar organizations in other fields—everything from dignified publicity to lobbying to prevent governmental discrimination against government programs involving alcoholism. The preamble to its "Principles of Practice," a statement of fundamental rules for members, is lofty but not pompous, wide-ranging but confined to its own territory of alcoholism; and it does not belabor the patriotic theme of what's good for the association is good for the country.

Among other points, it says treatment should be molded to meet the physical, emotional, social, and spiritual needs of each patient, and should include the family, employer, and "significant others"; it should aim at bringing out the patient's full potential and a better life; programs should "enhance the dignity and protect the human and legal rights of the patient by promoting self-respect, preserving individuality, and protecting the need for privacy and confidentiality"; and there should be strong aftercare efforts.

Quarreling with these objectives would be difficult and we can but hope and wish that all alcoholic treatment centers follow them. Some I know do not. In many cases the shortcomings are the result of what I would consider incompetent, un-understanding therapists. In the larger establishments, which have perhaps half-a-dozen or more staff therapists, they can influence one another, keep in check each other's egos and angers and frustrations. Actually one or two or three therapists can do every bit as well on their own, if they have the necessary sympathy, understanding, and humility.

These traits come more easily to the person who has been through the alcoholism mess himself. But more and more schools now are training students for alcohol and drug therapy and many seem to be successful. If they are, they can help meet what could become one of the major problems of expanded alcoholism treatment—finding enough qualified people to do the treating.

Alcoholism therapists do need something special. But it may be an innate quality rather than experience. One of the most successful people in the business has never been drunk in her young life and never has she had more than a token drink. Her training came almost accidentally when she was a regular medical nurse. She became deeply interested in the drunks she attended in her normal professional activities and soon began specializing, a serendipity for which perhaps several hundred lushes can be thankful.

Many would-be therapists do not like the work once they get into it. They can have any one of many reactions, from revulsion to impatience. They can become angry at the drunk's denial stage; they can become bored with the drunken-escapade stories; they can feel helpless at lack of progress; they can feel the excessive strain of trying desperately to help people reluctant to help themselves. Perhaps most common, they can become discouraged and exasperated at the patient's failure or refusal to see the sense and logic of what they are trying to do. In short, they do not have the required empathy, the dedication, the patience.

The empathy can be taught—to the person with the proper emotional makeup. It isn't easy, but neither is it impossible. Some rehabilitation centers will get scores of applications for therapists' jobs and, after single interviews, turn down nine out of ten candidates. Something is missing in most of the applicants, but the interviewers have a difficult time explaining precisely what it is. Composing job-requirement specifications for alcoholism therapists would not be simple; it might not be feasible.

The money-making considerations in the alcoholism business have attracted a surprising number of quick-cure operations, some of which can certainly be considered quackery. The difficulty is trying to figure out which are fakes.

Like placebos, the phony centers sometimes work on some types of people. All drunks can be divided into three groups. At one end are those who cannot be changed, cannot be rescued, no matter what is done to them. They will continue drinking when they are confined to hospital beds with terminal alcohol-related sicknesses. At the other extreme are those who really would like to be saved but who, for one reason or another, will not take the initiative; once somebody starts to work on them, they are comparative pushovers; they have round heels.

Between the two extremes are most of us alcoholics, ranging in difficulty from the toughest to the easiest.

Those at the easy end may well profit gloriously from what I might classify as a freak course. So what difference does it make what you or I think of the treatment? It worked and that's what it is all about.

But it almost certainly would not work on those of us in the troublesome middle.

The proliferation of alcoholism-treatment centers has inevitably brought with it a proliferation in methods of treatment. I have had personal experience with none of the far-out systems, but I have heard of some of them from presumably trustworthy people. Neither you nor I is in a position to categorize any of them as preposterous, ridiculous, or fraudulent because in some cases they are just about what some people need.

I was told of one establishment in New York City that specialized in patients who are deep into sado-masochistic sex. Treatment, according to my leather-jacketed friend, revolved around the usual whipping, punching, pinching, biting, and other painful abuses—used not as punishment for drinking, but as rewards for not drinking. Much was made of the fact that alcohol acts as an anesthetic and can take a good bit of the pleasure out of the S-M procedures. The basic idea seemed to be to emphasize S-M as a release, instead of alcohol. The conventional teachings of Alcoholics Anonymous were never mentioned. And if a patient had even one drink, he was not allowed to attend the clinic's next regular Saturday night party, which featured "slam dancing," a weird form of disco-type exercise in which the dancers slam into each other seemingly with the sole purpose of hurting one another. It sounds weird to us stodgy old people, but the person who gave me some of the details said it had done wonders for her; not only had she stopped drinking, she had discovered a new depth to her life and was engaged to one of the best slammers she'd ever known. He too was an alumnus of the institution, she said.

In another type of place, which seems to be more common, pain is used as a conditioning device; patients have access to booze, but every time they take a drink they get an electric shock or are poked with a red-hot strip of wire, or get some similar painful stimulus. Related techniques have apparently been tried to train persons to be controlled drinkers. They are taught to judge the amount of alcohol in their systems, and if they do not stop when they have enough they get electric shocks, thwacks across the knuckles, or some sort of unpleasant reminder they are being naughty. Of this process, the AMA's *Manual on Alcoholism* says "there is insufficient evidence as yet to propose such techniques as being generally applicable but they are worthy of legitimate scientific study. The safest goal remains abstinence."

I cannot recall finding anyone who honestly thinks he can make a true ethanol addict into a controlled or social drinker. Perhaps some day a way will be found, but unfortunately probably not while I am still around.

The programs based on associating alcohol with something unpleasant, such as electric shock, are generally lumped together as "aversion therapy." The theory is that if the association is thoroughly distasteful, the patient will build up a conditioned reflex against drinking and will want no part of it. Practitioners of aversion therapy quite naturally hark back to Pavlov's dogs, who were taught to associate a dinner bell with eating, until finally they would drool with anticipation when the bell rang, whether they got their meal or not.

Distinctly apart from the kookie versions of aversion therapy is one that is thoroughly respectable, seems to have been just as successful as most systems, and prides itself as being "medically oriented." It is used in Raleigh Hills Hospitals, operated by the Advanced Health Systems, Inc., in a number of cities around the country, most of them in the West. Other hospitals also use the system, but the Raleigh Hills group is probably the largest.

Details of the treatment change as circumstances and theories change, but the course revolves around a stint of about two weeks—usually twelve to thirteen days—in a Raleigh Hills hospital unit. If detoxification is required, alcohol is used in limited quantities to ease the patient through withdrawal; the amounts needed vary widely and rapidly and must be carefully controlled under medical supervision. The procedure is widely criticized by many experts, but Raleigh Hills contends it reduces the incidence of delirium tremens, lowers blood pressure and pulse rates, cuts the time required for detoxification, and virtually eliminates the need for putting patients under physical restraint.

When the patient is dried out, he is told exactly how the long-range treatment works, according to the Raleigh Hills officials. If he doesn't like the prospect, he can get out, unless, of course, he has been legally committed, when it becomes more difficult.

He is taken into what might be a typical aseptic hospital room except for two features: windows are blacked out and the walls are one gorgeous big bar, with shelves lined with bottles of all varieties of booze. The patient is then given an injection which has as its basic ingredient emetine, which induces nausea and vomiting. When the emetine begins to take effect, the patient is given five or six drinks of whatever he chooses from the almost unlimited supply with which he is surrounded. He gets sick, gets rid of the booze before his body can absorb it, and is thoroughly miserable.

After a day for R and R—rest and recovery—he is given a second treatment, with the number of drinks increased, often doubled, and the types of alcohol varied. He gets five or six such treatments, sometimes is given twenty drinks at the final sitting. A nurse keeps track of his blood pressure and pulse rate. Twenty-four hours after the last treatment, the patient is sent home. But he returns in perhaps three weeks for still another go-round, a "reinforcement" session. Usually half a dozen reinforcements are administered over a year. The exact number depends upon the patient.

Presumably the course builds up in the patient an abhorrence of alcohol that will stay with him. The Raleigh Hills people claim a success rate of between 60 and 70 percent, which is modest enough to be believable, but all such claims can be challenged, as I have pointed out earlier.

The system does for sure work on some people. One of Raleigh Hills' big boosters is Gale Storm, a movie actress of sorts during the 1940s, a featured player in two well-known television series and a singer who recorded several hit numbers. After years of occasional social drinking, she quite rapidly became an alcoholic; she was hospitalized several times, tried psychiatric treatment and Alcoholics Anonymous and finally went to Raleigh Hills and straightened out. She is, so far as is discernible, a true believer. So much so that she has done television commercials for Raleigh Hills.

Raleigh Hills also uses conventional therapy, psychiatry, and other counseling. But the focus of its treatment is that spotless room lined with whiskey bottles and "emesis basins," those pans used in hospitals for vomiting.

Objections to the system, among some of those learned in such matters, include the contention that a full-blown aversion cannot be built up in such a short course, concentrated though it may be. Another objection is the lack of scientific evidence that a genuine addiction can be overcome by conditioning. If it could be, the argument goes, many addicts would cure themselves as a result of the anguish they go through during hangovers or enforced withdrawal.

One of my earliest recollections of alcoholism in action involved one of the finest newspaper editors I have ever known. He was liked and respected by his colleagues and in my youthful way I idolized him in a professional sense. In a period of two or three years, however, he deteriorated into a hopeless bum. He lost his job, of course. And every morning, shortly after opening time, he would fumble his way into the bar of the National Press Club in Washington, carefully prop himself over an empty spitoon and order a drink—which he would promptly throw up. He would order another and perhaps a third with the same results. The fourth would usually stay down and he was again on his way. His misery was obvious. In my naïveté, I wondered why he didn't stop torturing himself by the simple expedient of giving up booze; he certainly would seem a prime example of a person who would build up on his own aversion to alcohol. But his addiction ended only when he died, in his early fifties.

Other objections to the aversion theory range from medical through psychological to social. Yet it works, probably on as many people as do more routine-type treatments. Maybe it does create an aversion sufficiently powerful to overcome an addiction. We may have no medical evidence that it does, but neither do we have proof that it does not. If the aversion is strong enough to make an alcoholic think twice before taking that disastrous first drink, it's good.

Or perhaps the treatment is such a physical and emotional experience that it jolts the patient back into the real world. He may well reason that he never wants to go through that again, even if it means giving up alcohol. I know that was a factor in my own ultimate reorientation; the last rehab center I was in was so bad, so miserable, that I promised myself never again to subject what was left of my psyche to such a pounding.

The trauma of a severe jolt can do the trick, without benefit of treatment. The son of a once-famous business and political figure was an excessive drinker. He was probably an alcoholic, although in those prehistoric days he was known simply as a drunk. Driving home from a raucus Long Island party, he had an accident in which his beautiful and delightful sister was permanently crippled. The young man never took another drink, so far as I know.

What may be the decisive element in the success of the aversion therapy is the feeling many patients have that finally somebody is doing something specific and direct to help them. Many alcoholics ask their doctors if there is some medication that will diminish the craving. Will vitamins help? What about hormones? What about some of the new wonder drugs, won't they work?

In what might be called the conventional rehabilitation center, there is little suggestion of medical treatment to alter drinking habits; once detoxification is completed, there is scarcely a hint of drastic hospital measures. The patient understandably can wonder if he has a disease, an illness, why is he not subjected to medical therapy?

During aversion treatment, he is. Conceivably, the idea alone might turn him around, might work the way placebos work in some instances and on some people. I don't mean to imply that aversion therapy is a placebo—I am simply talking about the effect it might have on the patient. One doctor, who has taken a deep interest in alcoholism, explained it this way: the ordinary patient these days is accustomed to action. No matter what is wrong, he gets antibiotics, or shots, or other medication, perhaps surgery or a special diet or radiation or something. And in aversion therapy, something physical is done. That can mean a great deal.

The aversion treatment merits attention because it is a distinctive form of therapy, it does seem to be getting increasing attention, and allowing for the uncertainty of statistics, it does seem to have a measurable success rate. I myself have talked with a number of people who went through the treatment and they swear by it. Those it did not work on, I, of course, have not met.

The most widely used system still seems to be the more-or-less conventional method based solidly on the principles of Alcoholics Anonymous, which I attempted to explain in general terms earlier in this book. It is preferred, I believe, by a majority of the experienced practitioners in the field of alcoholism.

It is used by what is generally considered one of the country's largest chain of commercial rehabilitation centers, run by the Comprehensive Care Corporation, with headquarters in Newport Beach, California. Unfortunately, my first-hand knowledge of Comprehensive Care's operations is limited. I asked to talk to officials, but the request wouldn't even be considered, I was told, until and unless I submitted an outline of the book and a list of questions I wanted answered, demands to which no self-respecting reporter could agree. In addition, I wouldn't know what I wanted to ask until I knew more about the organization.

Comprehensive Care Corporation appears to be commercially successful, as this is written, judging from newspaper accounts of stock splits and predictions of large increases in stock earnings. And generally, it seems to be well regarded by most of the experts to whom I have talked. It would seem to be a prime example of how money can be made from helping alcoholics. Which, from an alcoholic's viewpoint, must be a hopeful sign.

A medical breakthrough that will make all such types of treatment obsolete is possible. A specific cause and cure of drug addiction may be developed to replace the relatively clumsy and cumbersome treatments we now must rely on. But what we have, which itself took years to develop, is surprisingly good; more people should try it.

12

Proceed With Caution

Classifying drinkers—deciding whether a drinker has a problem or is simply enjoying himself—is difficult indeed, even for professionals in the field of alcoholism. It is not like sorting letters or programming a boxful of silicon chips.

Two people telephoned me on successive days with what was fundamentally the same problem. One was male, the other female. Both were planning marriage. Both said they drank but not much, and neither did their affianced. But both were afraid their targeted partners might become alcoholics in the future, and along with the marriage vows they wanted vows of total abstinence. Neither caller would be bound by the oaths—only the people they married. That understandably started strenuous arguments, so both wanted to know how they could spot incipient alcoholics.

I would sooner attempt to sex baby chickens. The demarcation lines between an occasional social drinker, a regular social drinker, a heavy social drinker, an "alcohol abuser," and a full-fledged alcoholic are sometimes indiscernible. And a drinker can shift from one category to another so quickly and with so little commotion that no change is noticeable.

So far as I know, little productive research has been done along these lines, but more on that later. A great many studies have been made into what constitutes hazardous drinking and what characteristics distinguish a true alcoholic. Less attention seems to have been devoted to which pleasure-drinkers are most likely to progress to alcoholism—for very good reason—nobody knows where to begin. An addiction at times seems to be spontaneous, no matter what's involved—alcohol, drugs, food, work, sex, or whatever.

Most of us have heard about, read about, or known instances in which GIs, exposed to quantities of cheap drugs in such places as Vietnam, have casually quit when they got back to normal living. I know of one young man who had been on everything, including alcohol and heroin. He had lived in Asia for many years, where he was able to afford large quantities of not only heroin but opium and cocaine and some I had never even heard of. But when he came home, he almost literally forgot to take drugs—they were expensive, hard to get, and simply too much trouble. For the two years he was home, he was clean as a surgeon's scalpel, about as much of an addict as my canary.

Identifying an addict after he becomes one sometimes is hard enough, but it is a walkover compared to predicting who will become an addict to what.

There are some guidelines which may be useful. They have been put together in the form of questions from conversations with all sorts of people involved, one way or another, in the alcoholism area. The questions assume that the "you" involved is not a teetotaler, not even a free-bending social drinker, but someone who so far drinks moderately and occasionally. The questions are not necessarily in the order of their significance because the significance will differ with different individuals. Here goes:

1. Although you drink reasonable amounts, do you feel you simply must have a snort or two at regular times—before or after lunch or dinner, after work, before bed?

2. Do you consider a couple of drinks essential to having a truly good time at a party, in the sack, or on vacation?

3. Do you look forward with anticipation to the next occasion which you feel will justify drinking?

4. Do you think up justifications for having a couple of slurps?

5. Do you have a hard time refusing a drink, especially if it is pushed?

6. Is it difficult to resist peer pressure to take a drink?

7. Are you easily influenced by a drinking environment and drink because everybody else does?

8. Is it hard to stop after one or two?

9. Do you sometimes tell yourself you absolutely require a drink to relax?

10. Do you feel a strong need for alcohol after a period of unwonted tension—the death of someone close, a car accident, a grueling work session?

11. Do you sometimes simply crave a belt or two for no explicit reasons?

12. Do you need booze to fortify yourself for a tryst?

13. Do you need booze to fortify yourself for an experience you do not relish—going to a PTA meeting, making a public appearance, talking to the boss about a raise?

14. Is a drink needed to enjoy a movie, the ballet, sex?

15. Is a drink an essential ritual at a football game, for bowling, or after golf?

16. Do you feel the need of a drink to warm you after skiing or to cool you after a fast game of tennis?

17. Are you convinced, after drinking more than is your custom, that you are perfectly all right, can, for example, drive a car as well as anyone?

18. Do you feel no embarrassment, no regrets, that you were silly or loud or truculent, and excuse everything on the theory "I had a little too much"?

19. Do you feel, consciously or otherwise, that drinking is glamorous?

20. Do you like the feeling alcohol gives you?

✳ ✳ ✳ ✳ ✳

These questions undoubtedly do not cover the entire field, but perhaps they may start a few wheels turning. Affirmative answers can mean you already have a measure of dependence on alcohol; do not have the strength to say no; you think it is the thing to do; and/or you just plain like to drink. If you answer yes to four or five of the questions, you probably should be very careful. At the first sign of excess you should slow down or stop. You should monitor yourself, the way a heart patient monitors his ticker. Most people with a tendency toward true alcoholism will probably be inclined to ignore warning signals, the way a long-distance driver begins to ignore "dangerous curve" signs until he slams into a tree. You are the only person in the world who really knows what you really are doing, and it is much easier to get an honest answer out of yourself before you become an alcoholic than after.

Skipping from the potential alcoholic to the confirmed alcoholic—what might be considered irregular, unorthodox behavior is probably the most reliable indicator. But a doctor, for example, won't see enough of the patient to recognize these symptoms. The American Medical Association in its *Manual on Alcoholism* has a summary of characteristics that should lead a physician to suspect alcoholism. The list can be of equal value to co-workers and bosses and relatives and friends in trying to decide whether to close in on a possible drunk. The manual says a doctor should consider alcoholism if the patient has a history of:

1. An increasing use of alcohol, whether regular or occasional, along with frequent and "perhaps unintended" drunkenness.

2. The use of booze in dealing with problems or for relieving discomfort, presumably either physical or mental.

3. Preoccupation with booze and the repeated desire or need for a drink.

4. Sneaking drinks or gulping them down rather than having them for conviviality.

5. Making excuses, offering feeble "reasons," for drinking.

6. Refusing to concede that he drinks too much and getting irritated when the question is brought up.

7. Frequently missing work, particularly if absenteeism follows a pattern, usually coming after weekends and holidays—what the experienced supervisor knows as "Monday morning flu."

8. Frequent changes in jobs, especially if they go in a downward direction to levels lower than the patient's abilities and qualifications.

9. Shoddy appearance, poor hygiene, and substandard behavior.

10. Constant complaining about not being able to sleep, lack of appetite, stomachaches, headaches—with no apparent causes.

11. Frequent appeals for medical help for troubles that obviously involve alcohol.

12. Severe marital and family difficulties.

13. Repeated confrontations with police for drunkeness or drunken driving.

The AMA has also outlined, in various publications, other helpful hints for the doctor, many of them purely medical. But there are scores—perhaps hundreds—of additional factors, having little to do with medicine, that may indicate alcoholism. Some of these are repeats of points previously made, by way of emphasis; many are the result of somber academic studies; others are obvious generalities. Anyhow, here are some questions to ask yourself or someone you think may be over the cliff:

1. Can you stop drinking after consuming a reasonable amount?

2. Do you need a drink to strengthen your self-confidence to get through trying situations?

3. Do you ever have a genuine craving for alcohol?

4. Do you drink to get drunk?

5. Do you make flimsy excuses for drinking?

6. Do you use any handy "reason" for drinking?

7. Do you repeatedly decide to quit?

8. Do you drink surreptitiously and alone?

9. Do you drink in the mornings?

10. Do you feel a desperate need for a drink at regular times, such as before bedtime?

11. Do you neglect your personal appearance and personal business, such as paying bills, because of drinking?

12. Do you repeatedly do idiotic things which you regret?

13. Do you attempt to set limits on your drinking,

such as none before lunch or dinner, or only vodka or beer or wine?

14. Do you get in fights when drinking?

15. Do you lose time from work because of drinking?

16. Do you need alcohol to finish your work?

17. Do you drink to ease the pain of personal problems?

18. Is buying booze a financial problem?

19. Do you drink more than your friends?

20. Do you have memory blackouts?

21. Do you avoid the subject of drinking?

22. Do you resent any implication that you drink too much?

23. Have you lost friends as you continued drinking?

24. Have friends or family ever attempted to cut down your drinking?

25. Have you often been told you drink too much?

26. Have your bosses complained about your drinking?

27. Have you ever been fired or arrested or had an automobile accident where drinking was involved?

28. Do you have the shakes?

29. Have you been told that, when you drink, you talk Glish—(which isn't quite English and makes no sense whatever)?

30. Would you tell the truth in answering these questions and assessing yourself?

The list could go on for pages. Answers of "yes" obviously would establish a presumption of alcoholism.

Perhaps the most important question, if any one is more important than the others, is the last: would you tell yourself the truth in assessing yourself? One friend, for whom I compiled a list of questions like the above, was astonishingly candid with himself. The list wasn't quite as long, but he answered yes to every question. When he got through, he still insisted vehemently that he was not an alcoholic and could quit any time without pain or difficulty. I gave up. He did not quit drinking, although he lost his job and his wife and had ghastly money problems.

The idea of a questionnaire is not meaningless gamesmanship. It gives others—family and friends—definite information on which to work. Also some faint glimmer of truth may penetrate the most saturated alcoholic and soften him up a bit, though he denies every implication of the questions.

Perhaps the most revealing attitude I have encountered was with the great comedian and great personality, W. C. Fields. At a lunch with Fields and a mutual friend, I decided to have a martini, as did the friend. Fields rejected the idea, said he was on the wagon. But when the waiter came, Fields ordered a double slug of alcohol—I have long since forgotten what it was. I was startled and blurted out, "I thought you were on the wagon."

"I am," he answered, "I gave up martinis."

13

What to Do?

Alcoholism is as much a menace as drug addiction—physically, mentally, morally, socially, economically—almost any "ly" you can think of including statistically.

The media, a convenient but somewhat pompous noun, are brimming with stories about the perils of drugs but relatively rarely do they have sensational, slam-bang exposés on the hazards of alcoholism. If an automobile driver involved in a fatal accident is drunk, it's treated almost routinely, especially in the big cities; but if he is found to be under the influence of a drug, anything from tranquilizers to hallucinogens, the headline almost automatically doubles in size and prominence. Yet the victims are just as dead in one accident as the other. The driver at fault is just as far out of it in one accident as the other, and just as reprehensible. Once many years ago, before I became an alcoholic, I said on radio (before television) that a drunk who kills another with a car was as guilty as the person who uses a gun or knife or a club; only the weapon is different. The screams from angry listeners penetrated even the insulated executive offices of NBC in New York. NBC, by the way, backed me up.

In common usage, the word "drugs" does not encompass alcohol, although it should. "Drugs" are usually considered far more sinister. In my younger days a drug addict was too often thought of as a slobbering, snarling, maniac with bloody fangs hanging out of his mouth like walrus tusks. An alcoholic, on the other hand, is commonly pictured as a red-nosed, overweight, slovenly, comedic character barely able to hang on to a lamppost. Yet both are demented, neither is rational, neither will make sense, both are totally irresponsible, and both need help.

Alcohol has a pernicious glamour that even the mildest drugs cannot match. On television we see the most respectable personalities in dramas, situation comedies, and soap operas dallying with what are supposedly cocktails. We see beautiful women and strong, silent males about to savor magnificent wines. And we watch while macho sports stars and sinewy, leather-faced cowboys show us that beer is the be-all and end-all of good living. This does not mean advertising, whether in print or on television, makes alcoholics. It does not. But it demonstrates the difference in public attitudes toward alcohol and drugs. Shots of lovely women and sophisticated men happily snorting cocaine or mainlining heroin are, so far as I know, rather rare.

The young particularly are exposed to the glamorization of alcohol by their peers—and by their families. Their parents, suffering from explosive hangovers, talk gleefully about what a great party it was and delight in re-running the highlights. Wasn't it the funniest thing you ever saw when Joe fell into the fireplace and busted the coffee table? Did you ever see anything so hilarious as Mabel stripping and trying to do a hula?

The only point of all this is the belief that the first step in reducing alcoholism would be its deglamorization. Controlled drinking can be thoroughly enjoyable. Would I could do it. But alcoholism is not fun, nor is it glamorous. The alcoholic is a drug addict and it probably is as difficult for him to kick the habit as it is for the junky to kick his. And often as dangerous medically.

At the same time, alcoholism should be destigmatized; as has been explained, an alcoholic should not be considered a pariah, but a sick person who should be treated.

Alcoholism and drug addiction should get equal public billing as problems. Alcoholism could be greatly diminished if it were given the concern and publicity attracted by drug use. Great progress has been made in this direction since 1935, when two alcoholics—a surgeon and a New York broker—got together in Akron, Ohio, and generated what became Alcoholics Anonymous. The movement got a significant push in 1943 when the Yale University Center of Alcoholic Studies held its first Summer School of Alcoholic Studies; from the school came, among other good things, the ideas that led to the creation of the National Committee for Education on Alcoholism, which in turn grew into the National Council on Alcoholism. Another spurt, in large part engineered by former senator Harold Hughes, the Iowa Democrat, was the establishment in 1970 of the National Institute on Alcohol Abuse and Alcoholism. Hughes, a deeply religious man, is a splendid example of the recovering— recovered— alcoholic whose devotion to helping others has given the movement clout. A burly pile of muscle, a former trucker, gentle but tough and outspoken, Hughes went from the alcoholic bottom to the top in politics, public service, and in the spiritual work to which he dedicated much of his life.

Hughes symbolizes perhaps the most important factor in the change in attitude toward, and the increased interest in, the treatment of alcoholism as an illness. The courage of the Hughes, the Betty Fords, the Wilbur Mills, the Dick Van Dykes, and scores of others has done more to take the disgrace out of alcoholism, and to publicize it as an ailment that can hit anyone, than would any number of high-powered advertising campaigns.

One very prominent public figure I knew quite well actually was afraid and probably ashamed for several years to admit he was sober. But so far as I know, none of the alcoholics who went public suffered for their honesty, although some in Alcoholics Anonymous resented a magazine article by Wilbur Mills on his wrestling match with alcohol. The principal objections seemed twofold: Mills had violated the anonymity of AA, and there was always a chance he would have a relapse and thus bring ridicule and notoriety to the fellowship. The idea that he might have benefited thousands was too often considered irrelevant.

More Mills—and Fords and Van Dykes and Senator Talmadges and Billy Carters—are needed; people with the strength and honesty to admit what's wrong with them. It's one of the few ways alcoholism can get attention commensurate with the public agitation over drug use.

We should, of course, have standard campaigns to prevent and treat alcoholism. But with them must come the utilization of every other device to dramatize the fight.

Scare tactics and flamboyant Carrie Nation methods probably will do little good. And trying once more to eliminate alcohol, rather than alcoholism, would be a heinous mistake.

The medical profession can make a mighty contribution, starting with medical schools. The U.S. National Institute on Drug Abuse, whose work is bureaucratically entwined with that of the National Institute on Alcohol

Abuse and Alcoholism, says that in 1980, the number of medical school graduates was 14,393. The shiny new doctors came out of 122 medical schools and of these schools, says the institute, "few . . . offered courses in drug abuse or alcoholism." There is no breakdown on how many of the "few" put heavier stress on drug abuse than on alcoholism, but it doesn't really matter. Alcoholism is accustomed to being at the end of the line.

In 1971, the federal government began trying to get curricula in drug abuse and alcoholism in every medical school; as part of the program, school faculties would be helped in establishing courses in the diagnosis and treatment of alcoholism and drug problems, and in teaching the proper use of legal drugs. There could be no master plan. Each school would require a plan fitting its own traditions, operating methods, and basic philosophy. Each acceptable plan would be subsidized with a grant of $50,000—half of it to go to a career teacher who would head the program, and half for such incidentals as secretarial assistance, consultant fees, and travel expenses. It was a modest program, but measured in terms of the good it might do, it was one of the biggest bargains since the Louisiana Purchase. The only strenuous complaints I have heard about the effort is that it was too small. As of this writing, what there is of it is threatened of course by budget cuts and presumably will disappear entirely.

As of January 1980, sixty such career teacher grants had been awarded and the teachers given specialized training. Some of the sixty school programs were more effective and more beneficial than others, and only about one-half of the country's medical schools were involved. A handful of schools already had their own programs. But the figures all can be distilled into one simple fact: too many medical schools still do not offer courses in alcoholism as an illness, as a medical entity.

Various involved federal agencies also managed to get selected questions on alcoholism and drug use included in the National Board of Medical Examiner's examinations, taken by 90 percent of all medical students. It sounds simple but actually is an accomplishment roughly the equivalent of a chipmunk killing a hawk. Still another significant development was the encouragement of education in alcoholism and drug abuse for nurse practitioners and physicians' assistants.

(In 1978, the federal government spent approximately $300 million on all phases of alcoholic treatment, research, prevention and training. This figures out roughly to 5 to 10 percent of the actual annual economic cost of alcoholism.)

The most urgently needed missionary work is among the nation's actively practicing physicians, of which there are an estimated 364,000. A miniscule number know beans about alcoholism; almost all are limited by ignorance of the problem, a great many by antiquated theories and prejudices, a substantial number by bias arising from their own affection for alcohol. These are among the reasons the AMA's *Manual on Alcoholism* should be considered an outstanding achievement. It does make available the basic facts.

The average physician needs enlightenment on alcoholism almost as much as does the general public. The doctor has one advantage over the ordinary guy or gal—in theory, he knows the physical consequences of alcoholism. But he makes so little use of the knowledge that he might as well not have it.

The AMA is moving on the problem, too hesitantly for some but nonetheless noticeably. In 1979, it approved a report by its Council on Scientific Affairs that, among other things, called for "reaffirming" that effective and comprehensive treatment for alcoholics "requires the involvement of a physician." That would seem to be like putting a French chef in charge of world series umpires, but the report goes on to explain a physician should be responsible for the medical management of the patient, while the substantial part of the actual treatment can be handled by non-medical people, which is how it already is done in most of the better rehabilitation clinics. Even in this limited capacity, many doctors would have to be more aware of an alcoholic's problems than they are now.

All this sounds much more critical of the physician than is intended. Today's doctor has to read, study, and work almost endlessly to keep up with developments in his field; as a matter of fact, a conscientious general practitioner probably cannot keep up, and even the most highly specialized has difficulty staying abreast in his own narrow area. And the treatment of alcoholism is a relatively new concept and does not seem to have the urgency of heart problems, for example.

On the other hand, the fundamental information a doctor needs to handle intelligently the problems of alcoholism is not detailed, complicated or obscure, as is evidenced by the fact that the AMA's *Manual on Alcoholism* sums it up in a hundred pages. A physician need not—probably should not—actually treat the disease. But he should know enough about it to recognize it, to realize it can cause serious symptomatic illnesses, and to send the patient to the proper place for treatment.

One very reputable doctor, who took the time and trouble to bone up on alcoholism, told me proudly that he can spot the illness without fail and invariably sends an alcoholic to Alcoholics Anonymous. I asked him if he followed through on the patient, to make sure the prescribed treatment worked. He answered impatiently that of course he did not; if the patient did not return to him, the doctor considered him "cured." If there had been any way of getting the statistics, I would have been willing to bet the good doctor that not more than one out of four of the patients hung in with AA to sobriety. They may have come back to the fellowship later, after they had bumped bottom. If they did not they probably are dead.

Nudging the medical profession into realizing and accepting its responsibilities in alcoholism detection will make other reforms easier. The setting and maintenance of standards for rehabilitation clinics and related operations, for instance, requires the combined skills of all involved disciplines and are essential for the success of such undertakings as the labor-management programs. Some states already have standards, but as alcoholic clinics increase in number, size, and patronage, their performances should be more skillfully, painstakingly, and uniformly monitored.

Several states do well now. Some states don't even pretend. Perhaps the worst conditions occur, however, in states which supervise in theory but not in reality. Such supervision in name only allows even the most unscrupulous and shoddy clinics to impress the unsuspecting by claiming state approval. Requirements more wisely drawn can be more acceptable politically, and more sternly enforced, with physicians' cooperation—if the physicians know what they're talking about. So can the training of personnel to handle alcoholics.

The public attitude toward the medical profession is reminiscent of an old saw about the difference between North and South in race relations. Its thrust was that in the North, blacks are loved as a group but hated as individuals; in the South, blacks are loved as individuals but hated as a group.

So Americans will rant about the incompetence of individual doctors but defend them as a group; conversely, they will almost idolize them as individuals but boil them in verbal oil for their group methods on such matters as fees, the adoption of new techniques, and their tendency to protect each other. But in the problem of alcoholism, physicians must be an integral part—both individually and collectively—whatever their popularity rating.

Psychiatrists and clergymen also must be prepared and persuaded to join the effort to ameliorate alcoholism. They should function perhaps less pervasively but no less importantly. Their contacts with alcoholics may be less physical but nevertheless critically useful in what might be called mental and spiritual ways.

As a generalization, it might be fair to say that the psychiatrists who have the best chance of success with alcoholics are those that have ventured beyond the rigid boundaries of pure Freudianism and have moved into short-term therapy, behavior modification, and "cognitive therapy." All these involve, in a much too generalized sense, efforts to change patients' attitudes and responses, and to strengthen their determination to get better.

They also involve giving the patients feedback—trying to guide them, rather than making them find their own way. It is my feeling that the alcoholic is a white mouse in a maze and to get out, he must not only understand himself more fully, but he must often be led and encouraged. This, feedback can do.

On a more earthy level, psychiatrists—like physicians—need a more extensive knowledge of alcoholism to avoid clumsiness that can be disastrous. During my own thrashing around, my wife finally prevailed upon me to see a highly recommended psychiatrist. In other words, she forced me into making the crucial decision that I needed help. At the first and only session, the psychiatrist told me that he thought my wife needed treatment more than I did. I don't know what he meant, nor why he said it, but even my lumpy mind recognized it as a gross and uncomprehending statement.

While I felt overwhelmingly ashamed of, and guilty about, the woes I had brought my wife, I also blamed her and used her as a rationalization for my drinking; it was typically twisted alcoholic thinking. Thus the psychiatrist fortified one of my principal alibis. For another, the psychiatrist knew my wife was already getting help to try to carry her through an impossible situation. But most important, he had turned me off completely, thus negating my admission that I should do something about myself. The bull in the china closet was an airy-fairy Tinker Bell compared to him.

If I attempted to go into detail on how psychiatrists could be more effective it would probably require a second volume of this book. Further, I most likely wouldn't ever truly know what I was talking about. But all psychiatrists have had medical training, and if they, like doctors in general, learn more about the subject in medical schools, they will be better equipped to handle it.

I would be equally handicapped in trying to figure out how clergymen could be better prepared. There are so many variations in the precepts of religious groups and my own ignorance is so profound that I wouldn't dare attempt a detailed sortie into the territory. It does seem obvious, however, that many men of the cloth need a deeper knowledge of the subject than they now have. It was encouraging to me that so many churches send their members to rehabilitation centers and to Alcoholics Anonymous. But that doesn't take care of the man in the pew.

Another area that needs attention is alcoholism research, and here again doctors must lead rather than sit by passively passing judgments. They must not only do research themselves but must give it direction. They must not only encourage it, but make use of its results. They must learn it is important rather than frivolous.

The research that has been done and is being done

has made invaluable contributions. Much of it has been directed toward learning what happens to alcohol in the bodies of lower animals and humans: how it is absorbed into the blood stream, where it goes then, and what effects it has on the brain, the heart, and other organs. Thus we know why a person's speech is slurred when he drinks too much, and why he cannot walk that cursed straight line; we learn just how his liver is thrown out of kilter, why he develops an ulcerated stomach, why he gets a blue-and-red balloon for a nose, why his hands shake.

Most of these studies are undoubtedly essential for a fundamental grasp of alcoholism. But now, perhaps, it is time to put the heavy emphasis on the question that even the glibest know-it-all cannot answer without challenge—the question of what causes alcoholism. Why can some people enjoy social, controlled drinking all their lives while others sooner or later will go over the cliff? Why can some who quit lose the craving—sometimes quickly, sometimes gradually—while others never get rid of it?

The prevailing theory about the causes, treatment, and prevention of alcoholism has been well summed up by Dr. Morris E. Chafetz, one of the founders of the National Institute of Alcoholism and Alcohol Abuse, head of the Health Education Foundation, holder of numerous other high positions and winner of all sorts of honors in the field.

Alcoholism research, he says, is as "complex as the population itself, because alcoholism affects members of all classes of society, all subpopulations, all ages, all geographical areas of the country." He then says the causes of alcoholism are probably biomedical only in a few cases, but rather are primarily psychological and social.

There is no disagreement over the fact that psychological and social problems can precipitate drinking—

problems of stress, loneliness, marital and job difficulties, insecurity, and all the others. Disagreement comes over whether these influences carry further and engender an addiction to alcohol.

Scholars distinguished in the study of alcoholism present persuasive arguments that there is a strong genetic factor in the illness. Many of their findings can be disputed on the grounds that they are not the results of scientifically controlled experiments, but rather are based on statistics—the same argument made by the tobacco industry to meet the original charges that cigarettes could cause lung cancer. Consider, for example, figures showing that children of alcoholic parents seem more likely to become alcoholics themselves than the children of nonalcoholic parents. These data have been countered by questions of how the children included in the compilation were selected, how it was determined (if it was) that the children of alcoholics did not get that way simply because of their exposure to alcohol or because of the tensions always present in an alcoholic household, or because the children accepted the alcoholic atmosphere as normal. Also, I have heard contrary figures indicating that children of alcoholic parents are sometimes so turned-off by their parents' behavior that they become ferocious teetotalers.

The dispute goes back and forth, with extremists on both sides. But there are indications that a predisposition to alcoholism may indeed be inherited, and the only intelligent way to settle the argument is by extensive, controlled and balanced study.

Still another area screaming for more research revolves around the question of whether alcoholism can be caused at least in part by subtle differences in body functions, and whether these differences might be present before the first drink is taken or whether they might be the result of drinking. Such "imbalances," if that's the correct word and it probably is not from a purist's standpoint, are already known to exist in some mental disturbances; they sometimes respond to medication.

So it is conceivable that the causes of alcoholism may be more biomedical than is generally conceded; addictions in general may be physiological as well as psychological. Those who support such a theory cannot be as positive as those who oppose it—because comparatively little research is available to give credence to their ideas, or suspicions or hunches. Perhaps their strongest support comes from unscientific sources—alcoholics who quit drinking and then mysteriously lose their craving. With some of them, it's not a matter of merely being able to fight off the desire for alcohol. It is rather a matter of not giving a damn about alcohol one way or the other. A vast majority of such people, I believe, share my own feeling. They do not intend to go back to booze because they are afraid the whole process might start over again. Some who do again try to dabble with drink find that is precisely what happens. Others may get away with it—if they don't go too far, don't drink too much, and can pull out of occasional relapses. No genuine alcoholic that I know about has ever succeeded in becoming a controlled social drinker; with most of us it is a question of all or nothing, alcoholism or abstinence.

As we learn more about what causes addiction to alcohol, if we do, we may develop more specific ways to prevent it. Preventive methods now are necessarily confined almost entirely to intangibles. Dr. William E. Bunney, of the National Institute of Mental Health, put it this way in the *New York Times*: "Future attempts at prevention are likely to remain oriented more to changes in the patient's lifestyle than his biochemistry."

Altering lifestyles is about as simple as turning lead into gold. But it is the only hope we have at the moment. Even a good many AA Twelfth Steppers—the first-aid teams that do such magnificent work in trying to help desperate alcoholics—are talking about "intervention"— the process of stepping in before an alcoholic scrapes himself raw on the bottom, rather than following the venerable AA axiom that he must first actively seek succor.

Ideally, prevention starts with the young, in some instances, the very young. Even when I thought alcohol was the nectar of the gods, I cringed when forced to be with parents who thought it was cute to give their toddlers a few sips of beer or wine or a highball. My wife and I were considered freaks when we lived in Paris because we would not let our children have the watered wine that French parents often feed their young almost from the time of weaning. I have long been convinced that an addiction to drugs can be triggered at the age of 2 as readily as at 22, and now it has been pretty well established that it can be started even before birth, if a mother is hooked.

North Carolina approached the prevention question by legislation; the state General Assembly in 1977 approved an effort to prevent a whole mess of things, including "the exorbitant social and economic costs of disease, deformities, and other human miseries." If such things could be handled by passing a law, it might solve most of the world problems.

A group of parents in DeKalb County, Georgia—one of six counties in the metropolitan area of Atlanta—took a more pragmatic approach, though the problem itself is amorphous. Shocked at the realization that their children were all mucked-up with the drug culture, members of the group decided to reassert themselves as parents by such old-fashioned methods as trying to understand more fully their children's problems and by imposing such non-chic rules as dating curfews, chaperoning, and punishments for drinking and drug use. By most accounts, it has had a worthwhile effect.

Such commendable exertions might be called "mass interventions," and while they may be ridiculed by some, they can do no damage and they may be beneficial. A ship may not always answer the rudder, but without a rudder there is no hope of steering it.

So at this point, the greatest hope for preventing alcoholism lies in altering the public concepts of the illness. The very idea of openly trying to compel a change in our attitude toward anything is repugnant to a properly independent people. It has an aura of Big Brotherhood, of unfashionable parental and pedantic authority; and it positively reeks of do-goodism. It is considered interference in our private business, which we as people have always resisted, sometimes violently. Ideally, programs should come from the roots, as in DeKalb County, Georgia. Once begun, they can be nourished by manipulative publicity, advertising, and political maneuvering. The hazards of alcohol and other drugs must be underlined but in a calm, convincing tone rather than hysterically. Reasonable limitations on the social use of alcohol must be clearly defined.

Mass intervention requires two basic devices—education and propaganda. Their uses and results are much alike and where one ends and the other begins is unimportant. In any organized campaign, they should probably first be employed no higher than state levels. The state is a relatively small, cohesive unit that usually can be handled as a unit. A state will, more often than not, take its communities along with it.

A state, for example, can set up, or help set up, mental health clinics where alcoholics and other drug addicts can go for guidance and treatment. The clinics can be manned by psychologists and counselors trained under state auspices. A foundation for state-level programs already exists in the National Association of State Alcohol and Drug Abuse Directors. Given more support and more attention, they could perhaps show more initiative and be a powerful force. Among other areas that might be more productive if more energetically cultivated is job placement for alcoholics who have had successful treatment. That gets into the private sector, which would profit most from a decrease in alcoholism. Private money, whether from industry, business or foundation-types, would get nice returns over the long haul if invested in sobriety.

The National Council on Alcoholism believes in, and has succeeded in, starting below the state level—at the community level. The methods and aspirations of the Council—the NCA—are worth a CAT-scan examination because they are well thought out by practical people who know what it is all about, know the difficulties and dangers as well as the opportunities in the field of alcoholism, and seem able to resist the self-hypnosis and narcissism that so often afflict high-minded private organizations as well as bureaucracies. In any major effort, the NCA's structure and operation might provide a blueprint and specifications for expanded construction.

Founders of the organization decided in 1944 that, from past experiences with cancer, heart disease, and tuberculosis, "it was clear that a new concept which faced deeply ingrained and emotional attitudes, could gain acceptance most effectively when leaders in a communtiy joined together to give it public support." The message of the NCA was succinct: alcoholism was a disease, alcoholics could be helped and were worth helping and alcoholism was a massive public health problem that demanded public action and attention.

On this sturdy foundation, the organization was growing with such enthusiasm that it had to cut the umbilical cord with its original sponsor, Yale University, and go out on its own. Now, according to my count, it has more than 220 local councils around the country affiliated

one way or another with the central office in New York—
everywhere from Tok, Alaska, to Fort Lauderdale, Florida.
As local councils increased, they drew the services, not
only of recovered alcoholics, but diverse and distinguished civic, business, and medical leaders. As a general
rule, these people can have only one motive — a desire to
help. All are volunteers, except of course the paid staff
people. The NCA is financed by contributions and membership fees, and cannot conceivably be classified as a fat
cat operation. Nor is it a route to the world of private
corporate jets and company-paid country club dues. It can
scarcely be considered a path to fame and glory and Nobel
prizes. More likely, its only substantial reward is the feeling of having done some good.

Yet the NCA now spreads across almost the entire
range of alcoholism. The national office lists eight depart-
ments and three professional components, each of which
operates in a different area. One function of the national
office is to help local communities provide the information
necessary to tell alcoholics and their families where to go
for what kind of assistance. Obviously, local groups are in
the best position to sort out what is available in their areas.
This function alone would make the NCA invaluable.

But the organization also promotes general education
on alcoholism, and it tries to make sure that the medical
and health professions assume and exercise their responsibilities in the treatment of alcoholics. Linked with these
endeavors is encouragement of research. NCA provides
support services and information to its three components—the Research Society on Alcoholism, the American
Medical Society on Alcoholism, and the National Nurses
Society on Alcoholism. The American Medical Society on
Alcoholism has more than a thousand members and
shines like a fluorescent needle in the medical haystack.

As a basis for a more extensive and intensive campaign against alcoholism, the NCA has things going for it

other than its comprehensive structure. It has had wide experience, beginning when anti-alcoholism was considered something between a mental quirk and a joke. It has dealt with the problem on the local, state, and federal level. It has dealt with business and unions, with minorities, with the medical and health professions, with the media, with practically all elements involved. I am sure it has detractors although I do not recall having met any. But it would be difficult to denigrate its concepts, its scope, and its sincerity.

I have run far off the baselines I marked out for myself when I began this venture, but I have done so with a feeling of security arising from the conviction that the vast majority of citizens are depressingly ignorant on the entire subject of alcoholism. There are countless self-crowned "experts" but precious few who can be considered experts without the quotation marks. Almost everyone who has been involved in alcoholism problems at any level tends to think he or she knows a great deal about the subject. But most of their expertise comes from the individual's own personal experiences, and as I have tried to make clear there are as many variations as there are people. I do not consider myself an expert, although I have spent months exploring as many alleys of alcoholism as I could find. In Tucson, Arizona, I still sit spellbound while a beautiful, very young and very intelligent woman tells me what she has learned in a decade of working with alcoholics. I am equally humble and muted when I have a chance to talk to a friend who is a wounded but not disabled veteran of literally hundreds of battles resulting from Twelfth Step missionary work for Alcoholics Anonymous. Listening to them is not good manners on my part. I am simply aware that the only thing I know for certain about alcoholism is that it is an unbelievably complicated subject and what I don't know far exceeds what I do know.

Yet I repeatedly am didactically lectured by someone

whose experience consists of having had a great aunt who regularly got soggy on cough syrup. One nice youth one night gave me a three-hour course in alcoholism, as a result of having attended four meetings of Al-Anon, the organization that does such a superb job of helping people deal with alcoholic families.

I do not mock these people. At least they have some grasp of some fundamentals. But they, too, demonstrate the abysmal lack of comprehension if they think a few incidents make them masters in the field. Among the more common manifestations of ignorance is the belief that the only hopes for successful treatment lie in physicians, psychiatrists, clergymen or Alcoholics Anonymous; rehabilitation centers are regarded with contempt, if they are regarded at all. I have tried to emphasize and clarify this fifth hope, tried to emphasize that rehabilitation is not the ultimate answer but it is the best we have yet for the toughest cases, those on whom the first four do not work at all, or whose "cures" are temporary. One of the most exasperating experiences in dealing with alcoholics is to have their friends and relatives surrender completely on the grounds that they've tried everything they could— doctors, shrinks, vicars and AA—and nothing has worked. A rehabilitation clinic cannot be guaranteed, but it's worth trying—once, twice, four times, as in my own case, or as many more as can be squeezed in while the patient is still breathing.

I have tried as best I could to get across the intricacies and to explain that neither the alcoholic nor those who want to give him a hand should give up hope until far after the point of hopelessness is reached. If I have succeeded with an appreciable number of people, I will be as happy as a clam at high tide. Or, as I prefer to put it, happy as a bull in Montana.

APPENDIX I

National Council on Alcoholism Affiliates

Member groups of the National Council on Alcoholism stand like cheerful information booths for anyone trying to find his way through the forbidding and confusing wilderness of alcoholism. Local NCA affiliates usually can point the harried traveler in the right direction, advise him how to keep on course, give him strength and psychological sustenance and alert him to some of the minefields ahead.

NCA headquarters in New York City has agreed to let me include a list of its affiliates. They go under different labels in different areas. The list includes the groups' names, addresses and phone numbers. Some may have changed but the list still will give clues on how they can be located. They can be reached in person, by phone or by letter. Most of the personnel have had significant experience in handling alcoholism problems.

ALABAMA

State Affiliate

NCA ALABAMA DIVISION, INC.
309 N. Hull Street
Montgomery, AL   36104
205/834-3614

Alexander City   REGIONAL ALCOHOLISM COUNCIL
                  OF CHAMBERS, LEE, RUSSELL &
                  TALLAPOOSA
                  424 Scott Road
                  Alexander City, AL 35010
                  205/329-8451

Birmingham   JEFFERSON-BLOUNT-ST. CLAIR
                  REGIONAL ALCOHOLISM COUNCIL
                  1211-28th Street, South
                  Birmingham, AL 35205
                  205/324-4676

Gadsden   REGIONAL ALCOHOLISM COUNCIL
                  OF DE KALB, CHEROKEE, ETOWAH
                  1000 Forrest Avenue
                  Gadsden, AL 35901
                  205/547-6903

Mobile   NCA-SOUTHWEST ALABAMA
                  COUNCIL ON ALCOHOLISM, INC.
                  962-A Government Street
                  Mobile, AL 36604

Montgomery   CENTRAL ALABAMA REGIONAL
                  COUNCIL ON ALCOHOLISM, INC.
                  1116 South Hull Street
                  Montgomery, AL 36104
                  205/262-7401

ALASKA

Akiachuk

AKIACHUK COUNCIL ON
  ALCOHOLISM
General Delivery
Akiachuk, AK 99551
907/543-2001

Anchorage

ANCHORAGE COUNCIL ON
  PREVENTION OF ALCOHOL AND
  DRUG ABUSE
7521 Old Seward Highway, Suite A
Anchorage, AK 99502
907/349-6602

Dillingham

BRISTOL BAY COUNCIL ON
  ALCOHOLISM AND DRUG ABUSE
P.O. Box 10235
Dillingham, AK 99576
907/842-5291

Ft. Yukon

FT. YUKON CITY ALCOHOLISM
  PROGRAM
P.O. Box 22
Ft. Yukon, AK 99740
907/662-2320

Juneau

GASTINEAU COUNCIL ON
  ALCOHOLISM
P.O. Box 568
Juneau, AK 99802
907/586-1688

Kenai

COOK INLET COUNCIL ON
  ALCOHOLISM
P.O. Box 882
Kenai, AK 99611
907/262-4220

Ketchikan GATEWAY COUNCIL ON ALCOHOLISM
628 Park Street
Ketchikan, AK 99901
907/225-6611

Kodiak KODIAK COUNCIL ON ALCOHOLISM
P.O. Box 497
Kodiak, AK 99615
907/486-3535

Petersburg PETERSBURG COUNCIL ON
ALCOHOLISM
P.O. Box 1066
Petersburg, AK 99833
907/772-3552

Seward SEWARD COUNCIL ON ALCOHOLISM
AND COMMUNITY SERVICES
P.O. Box 1045
Seward, AK 99664
907/224-5257

Sitka SITKA COUNCIL ON ALCOHOLISM
P.O. Box 963
Sitka, AK 99835
907/747-3636

Tok UPPER TANANA REGIONAL COUNCIL
ON ALCOHOLISM
P.O. Box 155
Tok, AK 99780
907/883-4201

Wrangell WRANGELL COUNCIL ON
ALCOHOLISM & RELATED DRUGS
P.O. Box 1108
Wrangell, AK 99929
907/874-3149

ARIZONA

Globe
GILA COUNCIL ON ALCOHOLISM,
INC.
115 West Oak Street
Globe, AZ 85501
602/425-4893

Phoenix
NCA, INC.-GREATER PHOENIX AREA
1515 East Osborn Road
Phoenix, AZ 85014
602/264-6214

Tucson
ALCOHOLISM COUNCIL OF
SOUTHERN ARIZONA
2302 E. Speedway, Suite 104
Tucson, AZ 85719
602/886-2576

Yuma
YUMA COUNTY ASSOCIATION FOR
BEHAVIORAL HEALTH SERVICES,
INC.
1355 W. 16th Street
Yuma, AZ 85364
602/782-4365

CALIFORNIA

State Affiliate

ALCOHOLISM COUNCIL OF CALIFORNIA/NCA
127 N. Madison, Suite 203
Pasadena, CA 91101
213/449-5611

Bakersfield
NATIONAL COUNCIL ON
ALCOHOLISM OF KERN
610 - 18th Street, Suite 5
Bakersfield, CA 93301
805/327-5758

Downey

SOUTHEAST COUNCIL ON
ALCOHOLISM & DRUG PROBLEMS,
INC.
11435 S. Downey Avenue
Downey, CA 90241
213/923-4545
585-0030

Fresno

ALCOHOLISM COUNCIL OF FRESNO
COUNTY
1651 "L" Street
P.O. Box 4616
Fresno, CA 93721
209/266-9888

Jackson

AMADOR COUNCIL ON
ALCOHOLISM, INC.
P.O. Box 338
206 North Main
Jackson, CA 95642
209/223-3802

Lancaster

ALCOHOLISM COUNCIL OF
ANTELOPE VALLEY
943 West Avenue "J"
Lancaster, CA 93534
805/948-5046

Loomis

SIERRA COUNCIL ON ALCOHOLISM &
ALCOHOL ABUSE
3390 Taylor Road, Space 29
Loomis, CA 95650
916/652-5831

Los Angeles

NATIONAL COUNCIL ON
ALCOHOLISM—LOS ANGELES
COUNTY, INC.
900 N. Alvarado Street
Los Angeles, CA 90026
213/413-4800

Branches

ALCOHOLISM COUNCIL OF SOUTH CENTRAL LOS
    ANGELES
Compton Project
215 South Acacia
Compton, CA 90220
213/774-8263

ALCOHOLISM COUNCIL OF EAST SAN GABRIEL AND
    POMONA VALLEY
955 N. Grand Avenue
Covina, CA 91724
213/331-5316

ALCOHOLISM COUNCIL OF SOUTH BAY
12345 Hawthorne Way
Hawthorne, CA 90250
213/644-3659

ALCOHOLISM COUNCIL OF GREATER LONG BEACH, INC.
330 East Third Street
Long Beach, CA 90802
213/432-3441

ALCOHOLISM COUNCIL OF GREATER EAST LOS
    ANGELES
916 So. Atlantic Boulevard
Los Angeles, CA 90022
213/724-3100

ALCOHOLISM COUNCIL OF SOUTH CENTRAL LOS
    ANGELES
8530 S. Vermont Avenue
Los Angeles, CA 90044
213/753-3243

ALCOHOLISM COUNCIL OF THE WEST AREA
1424 Fourth Street, Suite 205
Santa Monica, CA 90401
213/451-5881

ALCOHOLISM COUNCIL OF SOUTH BAY
1334 Post Avenue
Torrance, CA 90501
213/328-1460

ALCOHOLISM COUNCIL OF SAN FERNANDO VALLEY
6514 Sylmar Avenue
Van Nuys, CA 91401
213/997-0414

Pasadena

PASADENA COUNCIL ON
ALCOHOLISM, INC.
597 East Green Street, Suite 201
Pasadena, CA 91101
213/795-9127

Placerville

EL DORADO COUNCIL ON
ALCOHOLISM, INC.
50 Main Street
Placerville, CA 95667
916/622-8193

Riverside

ALCOHOLISM COUNCIL OF
RIVERSIDE COUNTY
3965 Merrill Avenue
Riverside, CA 92506
714/683-4950

Sacramento

NCA-SACRAMENTO COUNTY
AFFILIATE, INC.
2432 Glendale Avenue
Sacramento, CA 95825
916/485-4667

San Diego

NCA-GREATER SAN DIEGO AREA,
INC.
1140 Union, Suite 404 (92101)
P.O. Box 20852
San Diego, CA 92120
714/234-8494

San Francisco   NCA-BAY AREA, INC.
                         2655 Van Ness Avenue, Suite 370
                         San Francisco, CA 94109
                         415/563-5400

                         San Francisco Satellites

SOUTH ALAMEDA COUNTY INFORMATION CENTER
22300 Foothill Blvd., Suite 510
Hayward, CA 94541
415/881-0222

ALAMEDA COUNTY INFORMATION CENTER
360 - 29th Street, Suite 200
Oakland, CA 94609
415/834-5598

San Jose   NCA-SANTA CLARA COUNTY, INC.
                         100 N. Winchester Avenue
                         Suite 330
                         San Jose, CA 95128
                         408/241-6903
                             241-1771

Santa Ana   NCA/ORANGE COUNTY, INC.
                         2110 E. First Street
                         Suites 115-118
                         Santa Ana, CA 92705
                         714/835-3830

Santa Barbara   NCA-SANTA BARBARA AREA, INC.
                         P.O. Box 28
                         4570 Calle Real
                         Santa Barbara, CA 93102
                         805/964-4781

Santa Rosa   NATIONAL COUNCIL ON
                             ALCOHOLISM—SONOMA COUNTY
                         P.O. Box 2661
                         430 Montgomery Drive
                         Santa Rosa, CA 95405
                         707/544-7544

Tulare

NCA-TULARE COUNTY, INC.
P.O. Box 249—525 E. Bardsley Avenue
Tulare, CA 93275
209/733-0225
   733-2626

COLORADO

State Affiliate

ALCOHOLISM COUNCIL OF COLORADO
2525 W. Alameda Drive—Suite 219
Denver, CO 80219
303/922-6327

Boulder

BOULDER COUNCIL ON ALCOHOLISM
P.O. Box 2047
Boulder, CO 80302
303/443-4974

Colorado Springs

NCA-PIKES PEAK REGION, INC.
12 North Meade
Colorado Springs, CO 80909
303/634-3487
   633-4601

Denver

NCA-MILE HIGH AREA, INC.
2525 W. Alameda Drive, Suite 214
Denver, CO 80219
303/934-2101

Fort Morgan

MORGAN COUNTY COUNCIL ON
   ALCOHOLISM
c/o Steve Proctor, Chair
323 Apache
Fort Morgan, CO 80701
303/867-8268

Grand Junction

NCA-MESA COUNTY
761 Rood Avenue
Grand Junction, CO 81501
303/243-3140

CONNECTICUT

Bridgeport
GREATER BRIDGEPORT AREA
COUNCIL ON ALCOHOLISM
480 Bond Street
Bridgeport, CT 06610
203/366-5817

Cos Cob
THE ALCOHOLISM COUNCIL
521 Post Road
Cos Cob, CT 06807
203/661-9011

New Haven
ALCOHOL SERVICES ORGANIZATION
OF SOUTH CENTRAL CONNECTICUT
130 Park Street
New Haven, CT 06511
203/787-2111

Westport
ALCOHOLISM COUNCIL OF
MID-FAIRFIELD COUNTY
489 Post Road East
Westport, CT 06880
203/227-7644
226-0043

DELAWARE

State Affiliate

DELAWARE ALCOHOLISM COUNCIL, INC.
103 West 7th Street
Wilmington, DE 19801
302/656-8274

DISTRICT OF COLUMBIA

Washington, D.C.   WASHINGTON AREA COUNCIL ON
ALCOHOLISM & DRUG ABUSE, INC.
1221 Massachusetts Avenue, N.W.
Suite A
Washington, D.C. 20005
202/783-1300

FLORIDA

State Affiliate

FLORIDA CITIZEN'S COMMISSION ON ALCOHOL ABUSE,
INC./NCA
1018 Thomasville Road
Suite 104
Tallahassee, FL 32303
904/222-6314

Fort Lauderdale   BROWARD COUNTY COMMISSION ON
ALCOHOLISM, INC.
417 South Andrews Avenue
Fort Lauderdale, FL 33301
305/763-4505

Jacksonville   NORTHEAST FLORIDA COUNCIL ON
ALCOHOLISM & DRUG ABUSE, INC.
4355 University Boulevard, So.
Jacksonville, FL 32216
904/733-7444

GEORGIA

Atlanta   METROPOLITAN ATLANTA COUNCIL
ON ALCOHOL & DRUGS
2045 Peachtree Road, N.E.
Suite 320
Atlanta, GA 30309
404/351-1800

Macon
MIDDLE GEORGIA COUNCIL ON
    DRUGS
195 Holt Avenue
Macon, GA 31201
912/743-4611

Waycross
AREA DRUG ALCOHOLISM COUNCIL,
    INC.
100 Plant Avenue
Waycross, GA 31511
912/283-4897

HAWAII

Honolulu
HAWAII COMMITTEE ON
    ALCOHOLISM
200 North Vineyard Boulevard, Suite 503
Honolulu, HI 96817
808/524-1144

IDAHO

State Affiliate

IDAHO COUNCIL ON ALCOHOLISM, INC.
c/o Dr. John Wallace
833 Cairn Drive
Nampa, ID 83651
208/466-7061(o), 208/467-9518(h)

Boise
ADA COUNTY COUNCIL ON
    ALCOHOLISM
1615 W. State Street
Boise, ID 83702
208/344-7801

Coeur d'Alene

KOOTENAI COUNTY COUNCIL ON
  ALCOHOLISM
810 River Avenue
P.O. Box 735
Coeur d'Alene, ID 83814
208/667-9591

ILLINOIS

State Affiliate

ILLINOIS ALCOHOLISM
  & DRUG DEPENDENCE ASSOCIATION
401 West Highland Avenue
Springfield, IL 62704
217/528-7335

Charleston

CENTRAL EAST ALCOHOLISM &
  DRUG COUNCIL
635 Division
Charleston, IL 61920
217/348-8108

Decatur

THE ALCOHOLISM COUNCIL FOR THE
  DECATUR AREA
2490 North Water Street, Suite 11
Decatur, IL 62526
217/877-5263

East Moline

ROCK ISLAND COUNTY COUNCIL ON
  ALCOHOLISM
Route 2, Box 288
East Moline, IL 61244
309/792-0292

East St. Louis

ALCOHOLISM & DRUG DEPENDENCE
  COUNCIL OF ST. CLAIR COUNTY,
  INC.
2501 Ridge Street
East St. Louis, IL 62205
618/875-6300

Park Forest	SOUTH SUBURBAN COUNCIL ON ALCOHOLISM 2448 Western Avenue, Suite 10 Park Forest, IL 60466 312/481-9310 333-4357 747-1234
Peoria	CENTRAL ILLINOIS VALLEY ALCOHOLISM COUNCIL 5407 N. University Street Peoria, IL 61614 309/692-1766
Quincy	WESTERN ILLINOIS COUNCIL ON ALCOHOLISM 537 Broadway, Lower Level Quincy, IL 62301 217/224-7515
Springfield	SANGAMON-MENARD ALCOHOLISM & DRUG COUNCIL 614 South Grand Avenue East Springfield, IL 62703 217/544-3396
Waukegan	LAKE COUNTY COUNCIL ON ALCOHOLISM 1113 Greenwood Waukegan, IL 60085 312/244-4434

INDIANA

Elkhart	ELKHART COUNTY ALCOHOLISM COUNCIL 512 Communicana Building 421 South 2nd Street Elkhart, IN 46516 219/294-3981

Indianapolis   GREATER INDIANAPOLIS COUNCIL
ON ALCOHOLISM, INC./NCA
3052 Sutherland Avenue
Indianapolis, IN 46205
317/926-3756

South Bend   ALCOHOLISM COUNCIL OF ST.
JOSEPH COUNTY, INC.
521 ½ East Jefferson Boulevard
South Bend, IN 46617
219/234-6024

IOWA

Davenport   CENTER FOR ALCOHOL & DRUG
SERVICES, INC.
601 Brady Street
Suite 220
Davenport, IA 52803
319/322-2667

Des Moines   NCA-DES MOINES AREA, INC.
606 Fleming Building
Des Moines, IA 50309
515/244-2297

Iowa City   MID-EASTERN COUNCIL ON
CHEMICAL ABUSE
325 E. Washington
Iowa City, IA 52240
319/351-4357

Sioux City   SIOUXLAND COUNCIL ON
ALCOHOLISM & DRUG ABUSE
2825 Douglas Street
Sioux City, IA 51104
712/277-1163

KANSAS

Manhattan
THE RILEY COUNTY COUNCIL ON
ALCOHOLISM AND DRUG
EDUCATION, INC.
404 Humboldt, Suite C
Manhattan, KS 66502
913/539-7004

Topeka
NCA-KANSAS Division, INC.
1301 South Topeka Avenue
Topeka, KS 66612
913/233-0165
233-0205 (Employee Assistance)

KENTUCKY

State Affiliate

KENTUCKY ALCOHOLISM COUNCIL
629 Broadway, Suite 207
P.O. Box 868
Lexington, KY 40587
606/254-2761

LOUISIANA

Baton Rouge
ALCOHOL & DRUG ABUSE COUNCIL
OF GREATER BATON ROUGE, INC.
1819 Florida Boulevard
Baton Rouge, LA 70802
504/343-8330
383-1708

New Orleans
COMMITTEE ON ALCOHOLISM AND
DRUG ABUSE OF GREATER NEW
ORLEANS
3314 Conti Street
New Orleans, LA 70119
504/524-4357

Shreveport
CADDO-BOSIER COUNCIL ON
ALCOHOLISM, INC.
619 Market Street, Suite 413
Shreveport, LA 71101
318/222-8511

MAINE

State Affiliate

NATIONAL COUNCIL ON ALCOHOLISM
IN MAINE
128 State Street
Augusta, ME 04330
207/622-4704

Lewiston
WESTERN REGIONAL COUNCIL ON
ALCOHOL ABUSE & ALCOHOLISM,
INC.
P.O. Box 3068
179 Lisbon Street
Lewiston, ME 04240
207/783-9151

Rockland
PEN-BAY COUNCIL ON ALCOHOLISM,
INC.
Midcoast Mental Health Center
385 Main Street
Rockland, ME 04841
207/594-2541

Augusta   KENNEBEC-SOMERSET ALCOHOL
                   AND DRUG ABUSE COUNCIL, INC.
               P.O.B. 1038 (25 Drew Street)
               Augusta, ME 04330
               207/289-3411-ext. 25

MARYLAND

Easton   EASTERN SHORE COUNCIL ON
                   ALCOHOLISM, INC.
               P.O. Box 351
               Easton, MD 21601
               301/822-4133
                   822-5580

Hagerstown   WASHINGTON COUNTY COUNCIL ON
                   ALCOHOLISM, INC.
               310 Professional Arts Building
               Hagerstown, MD 21740
               301/790-2171

MASSACHUSETTS

Danvers   NORTH SHORE COUNCIL ON
                   ALCOHOLISM, INC.
               183 Newbury Street
               Danvers, MA 01923
               617/777-2664

Fall River   ALCOHOLISM COUNCIL OF GREATER
                   FALL RIVER
               P.O. Box 88
               Fall River, MA 02722
               617/675-0336

Hyannis   CAPE COD COUNCIL ON
                          ALCOHOLISM, INC.
                       349 Main Street, Room 8
                       Hyannis, MA 02601
                       617/771-0132

Nantucket Island   NANTUCKET COUNCIL ON
                          ALCOHOLISM
                       Gouin Village
                       P.O. Box 451
                       Nantucket Island, MA 02554
                       617/228-3655

Pittsfield   BERKSHIRE COUNCIL ON
                          ALCOHOLISM, INC.
                       214 Francis Avenue
                       Pittsfield, MA 01270
                       413/499-1000

Wollaston   SOUTH SHORE COUNCIL ON
                          ALCOHOLISM
                       148 Old Colony Avenue
                       Quincy, MA 02170
                       617/773-1380, Ext. 265, 266
                          472-6027—Hotline

Worcester   NATIONAL COUNCIL ON
                          ALCOHOLISM—GREATER
                          WORCESTER
                       9 Walnut Street, Room 211
                       Worcester, MA 01608
                       617/756-5163

MICHIGAN

State Affiliate

NATIONAL COUNCIL ON ALCOHOLISM, INC./MICHIGAN
2875 Northwind Drive, Suite 225
East Lansing, MI 48823
517/337-8417

Ann Arbor

WASHTENAW COUNCIL ON
ALCOHOLISM, INC.
2301 Platt Road
Ann Arbor, MI 48104
313/971-7900

Clare

MID-MICHIGAN COUNCIL ON
ALCOHOLISM, INC.
Human Aids, Inc.
104 East 7th Street
Clare, MI 48617
517/386-3405

Detroit

NATIONAL COUNCIL ON
ALCOHOLISM—GREATER DETROIT
AREA, INC.
1800 Kales Building
76 W. Adams
Detroit, MI 48226
313/963-0581

Flint

NCA-GREATER FLINT AREA, INC.
202 E. Boulevard Drive, Suite 350
Flint, MI 48504
313/767-0350

Holland

OTTAGAN ALCOHOLIC
REHABILITATION, INC.
P.O. Box 832-C
118 East 9th Street
Holland, MI 49423
616/396-6872, 396-5284

Kalamazoo

KALAMAZOO ALCOHOL & DRUG
ABUSE COUNCIL
814 West Kalamazoo Avenue
Kalamazoo, MI 49007
616/345-2139

Lansing

NCA-LANSING REGIONAL AREA, INC.
111 West Mt. Hope
Lansing, MI 48910
517/482-1417

Muskegon

MUSKEGON COUNTY COUNCIL ON
    ALCOHOLISM, INC.
402 Frauenthal Building
Muskegon, MI 49440
616/722-1931 or 7550

Saginaw

SAGINAW COUNTY INFORMATION
    CENTER ON ALCOHOLISM, INC.
2216 Weiss Street
Saginaw, MI 48602
517/792-2943

MISSISSIPPI

Jackson

NCA OF CENTRAL MISSISSIPPI AREA,
    INC.
1510 North State Street, Suite 202
Jackson, MS 39202
601/354-3253

MISSOURI

Kansas City

NCA-KANSAS CITY AREA, INC.
6155 Oak Street, Suite C
Kansas City, MO 64113
816/361-5900

St. Louis

ST. LOUIS AREA/NATIONAL COUNCIL
    ON ALCOHOLISM, INC.
7438 Forsyth Street, Suite 206
St. Louis, MO 63105
314/721-7225

MONTANA

State Affiliate

NCA-MONTANA
2033 11th Avenue
Helena, MT 59601
406/442-5726

Butte

BUTTE INDIAN ALCOHOLISM
    PROGRAM
2 East Galena
Butte, MT 59701
406/792-0461

NEBRASKA

State Affiliate

ALCOHOLISM COUNCIL OF NEBRASKA/NCA
215 Centennial Mall South
Suite 412
Lincoln, NE 68508
402/474-0930

Grand Island

CENTRAL NEBRASKA COUNCIL ON
    ALCOHOLISM, INC.
302 Masonic Building
Grand Island, NE 68801
308/384-7365

Hastings

SOUTH CENTRAL COMMUNITY
    MENTAL HEALTH CENTER
P.O. Box 50
Hastings, NE 68901
402/463-5684

Lincoln

LINCOLN COUNCIL ON ALCOHOLISM
& DRUGS, INC.
212 Lincoln Center Building
215 Centennial Mall South
Lincoln, NE 68508
402/475-2694

Omaha

OMAHA COUNCIL ON ALCOHOLISM,
INC.
2222 California Street
Omaha, NE 68102
402/345-4080

NEVADA

State Affiliate

NCA/NEVADA
165 North Carson Street
Fallon, NV 89406
702/423-6048

Fallon

CHURCHILL COUNCIL ON
ALCOHOLISM & OTHER DRUGS
165 North Carson Street
Fallon, NV 89406
702/423-6048

NEW HAMPSHIRE

State Affiliate

NCA-NEW HAMPSHIRE
20 Hanover Street, Office No. 4-5
P.O. Box 726
Manchester, NH 03101
603/625-4528

NEW JERSEY

Burlington

BURLINGTON COUNTY COMMUNITY
ACTION PROGRAM ALCOHOLISM
PROGRAM & CENTER
La Gorse Square, Route 130
Burlington, NJ 08016
609/386-5800

Flemington

HUNTERDON COUNCIL ON
ALCOHOLISM, INC.
8 Main Street
Flemington, NJ 08822
201/782-3909

Lakewood

NATIONAL COUNCIL ON
ALCOHOLISM OF OCEAN COUNTY,
INC.
528 River Avenue
Lakewood, NJ 08701
201/367-5515

Montclair

NCA-NORTH JERSEY AREA, INC.
60 South Fullerton
Montclair, NJ 07042
201/783-9313

Red Bank

NCA OF CENTRAL JERSEY, INC.
157 Broad Street
Red Bank, NJ 07701
201/741-5200

Somerville

SOMERSET COUNCIL ON
ALCOHOLISM, INC.
104 Rehill Avenue
Somerville, NJ 08876
201/722-4900

Trenton

MERCER COUNCIL ON ALCOHOLISM
548 Bellevue Avenue
Trenton, NJ 08618
609/396-5874, 75

NEW MEXICO

Albuquerque

NCA-ALBUQUERQUE AREA, INC.
126 Washington, S.E.
Albuquerque, NM 87108
505/268-6216

Los Alamos

LOS ALAMOS COUNCIL ON
   ALCOHOLISM
P.O. Box 829
Los Alamos, NM 87544
505/662-5000

NEW YORK

Binghamton

BROOME COUNTY COUNCIL ON
   ALCOHOLISM, INC.
89-91 Court Street
Binghamton, NY 13901
607/723-7529

Buffalo

BUFFALO AREA COUNCIL ON
   ALCOHOLISM, INC.
245 Elmwood Avenue
Buffalo, NY 14222
716/853-0375

Corning

CORNING AREA COUNCIL ON
   ALCOHOLISM, INC.
139 Chemung Street
Corning, NY 14830
607/937-5156, 57

Elmira   ALCOHOLISM COUNCIL OF
                          CHEMUNG COUNTY, INC.
                          ALCOHOL INFORMATION CENTER
                          215 West Water Street
                          Elmira, NY 14901
                          607/734-1567

Ithaca   ALCOHOLISM COUNCIL OF
                          TOMPKINS COUNTY, INC.
                          109 West State Street
                          Ithaca, NY 14850
                          607/273-5422

Jamestown   CHAUTAUGA COUNTY COUNCIL ON
                          ALCOHOLISM
                          Roberts Building-West 3rd Street
                          Jamestown, NY 14701
                          716/664-3608

Branch Office

CHAUTAUGA COUNTY COUNCIL ON ALCOHOLISM
329-331 Washington Avenue
Dunkirk, NY 14048
716/366-4623
     366-4624

Mineola   LONG ISLAND COUNCIL ON
                          ALCOHOLISM, INC.
                          1505 Kellum Place
                          Mineola, NY 11501
                          516/747-2606

Satellite

LONG ISLAND COUNCIL ON ALCOHOLISM, INC.
2 Library Avenue
Westhampton Beach, NY 11978
516/288-6655

Mt. Morris   LIVINGSTON-WYOMING COUNCIL
ON ALCOHOLISM, INC.
The Livingston Campus
Mt. Morris, NY 14510
716/658-2881, Ext. 19

New City   ROCKLAND COUNCIL ON
ALCOHOLISM
c/o Voigt, 537 So. Mountain Road
New City, NY 10956
914/634-6716

New York   NEW YORK CITY AFFILIATE, INC.
133 East 62nd Street
New York, NY 10021
212/935-7075
     935-7070 Hotline
Executive Director: Allan Luks

Niagara Falls   NIAGARA COUNTY COUNCIL ON
ALCOHOLISM
644–16th Street
Niagara Falls, NY 14301
716/282-1228

Norwich   COUNCIL ON ALCOHOLISM FOR
CHENANGO COUNTY, INC.
P.O. Box 328
6 Turner Street
Norwich, NY 13815
607/334-5225

Rochester   NCA-ROCHESTER AREA, INC. HEALTH
ASSOCIATION OF ROCHESTER &
MONROE COUNTIES, INC.
973 East Avenue
Rochester, NY 14607
716/271-3540

Schenectady

ALCOHOLISM COUNCIL OF
　SCHENECTADY COUNTY, INC.
277 State Street, Room 314
Schenectady, NY 12305
518/382-3387

Syracuse

ONONDAGA COUNCIL ON
　ALCOHOLISM
700 Wilson Building
306 South Salina Street
Syracuse, NY 13202
315/471-1359
　　471-1373

Utica

NCA-ONEIDA COUNTY, INC.
42 Genessee St.
New Hartford, NY 13413
315/732-6155

White Plains

NCA-WESTCHESTER
10 Longview Avenue
White Plains, NY 10601
914/946-1358

Satellite

NCA-WESTCHESTER
35 Main Street
Mt. Kisco, NY 10549
914/666-8981

NORTH CAROLINA

State Affiliate

NCA-NORTH CAROLINA
518 West Jones Street
P.O. Box 10465
Raleigh, NC 27605
919/832-9625

Charlotte

CHARLOTTE COUNCIL ON
  ALCOHOLISM, INC.
100 Billingsley Road
Charlotte, NC 28211
704/376-7447

Durham

DURHAM COUNCIL ON
  ALCOHOLISM, INC.
Professional Building
1200 Broad Street, Suite G-5
Durham, NC 27705
919/286-4441

Morganton

BURKE COUNTY COUNCIL ON
  ALCOHOLISM
309 N. Sterling Street
Morganton, NC 28655
704/433-1221

Raleigh

RALEIGH-WAKE COUNTY COUNCIL
  ON ALCOHOLISM, INC.
3824 Barrett Drive, Suite 103
Raleigh, NC 27609
919/821-7515—Information
    821-7650—Treatment Center

OHIO

State Affiliate

OHIO ASSOCIATION
  FOR ALCOHOLISM PROGRAMS
700 Bryden Road
Room 219
Columbus, OH 43215
614/464-1985

Cincinnati

COUNCIL ON ALCOHOLISM OF THE
  CINCINNATI AREA, INC.
125 William Howard Taft Road
Cincinnati, OH 45219
513/281-7880

Cleveland

ALCOHOLISM SERVICES OF
   CLEVELAND, INC.
3030 Euclid Avenue
Cleveland, OH 44115
216/391-2300

Columbus

COLUMBUS AREA COUNCIL ON
   ALCOHOLISM
360 South Third Street, Suite 306
Columbus, OH 43215
614/252-2143

Hamilton

ALCOHOLISM COUNCIL OF BUTLER
   COUNTY OHIO, INC.
111 Buckeye Street
Hamilton, OH 45011
513/868-2100

Warren

TRUMBULL COUNTY COUNCIL ON
   ALCOHOLISM, INC.
Riverside Medical Arts Center
1296 Tod Place, N.W., Suite 100
Warren, OH 44485
216/392-2561, 545-2986

OKLAHOMA

Bartlesville

WASHINGTON-NOWATA COUNTIES
   COUNCIL ON ALCOHOLISM
1312 W. Hensley Boulevard
Bartlesville, OK 74003
918/336-2110

Oklahoma City

OKLAHOMA CITY COUNCIL ON
   ALCOHOLISM
P.O. Drawer 837
127 N.W. 5th Street
Oklahoma City, OK 73101
405/236-8449

Tulsa

TULSA COUNCIL ON ALCOHOLISM,
    INC.
Parkland Plaza Building
2121 South Columbia Avenue, Suite 470
Tulsa, OK 74114
918/749-6476

OREGON

State Affiliate

OREGON STATE COUNCIL ON ALCOHOLISM
P.O. Box 12547
Salem, OR 97309
503/370-8628

Corvallis

BENTON-LINN COUNCIL ON
    ALCOHOL & OTHER DRUGS
227 S.W. 6th Street
Corvallis, OR 97330
503/752-7982

Grants Pass

JOSEPHINE COUNTY COUNCIL ON
    ALCOHOLISM
714 N.W. "A" Street—Room 212
Grants Pass, OR 97526
503/476-9165

Klamath Falls

KLAMATH COUNCIL ON ALCOHOL &
    DRUGS
5160 Summers Lane
Klamath Falls, OR 97601
503/882-7211

Madras

JEFFERSON COUNTY COUNCIL ON
    ALCOHOL
639 "D" Street
Madras, OR 97741
503/475-6575

Ontario
MALHEUR COUNTY ALCOHOL &
DRUG AUTHORITY
611 S. Oregon
Ontario, OR 97914
503/889-2490

PENNSYLVANIA

Bethlehem
BETHLEHEM COUNCIL ON
ALCOHOLISM, INC.
Community Chest Building
520 East Broad Street
Bethlehem, PA 18018
215/867-3986

Butler
BUTLER COUNTY COUNCIL ON
ALCOHOLISM, INC.
227 South Chestnut Street
Butler, PA 16001
412/287-5294

Doylestown
BUCKS COUNTY COUNCIL ON
ALCOHOLISM, INC.
120 Green Street
Doylestown, PA 18901
215/345-6644
757-1560

Gettysburg
ADAMS COUNTY COUNCIL ON DRUG
& ALCOHOL ABUSE, INC.
108 Rear No. Stratton Street
Gettysburg, PA 17325
717/334-8154

Lancaster
NCA-LANCASTER COUNTY, INC.,
COUNCIL ON ALCOHOLISM &
DRUG ABUSE
630 Janet Avenue
Lancaster, PA 17601
717/299-2831

Media

ALCOHOLISM COUNCIL OF
    DELAWARE COUNTY, INC.
12 South Avenue
Media, PA 19063
215/566-8143

Philadelphia

NCA-DELAWARE VALLEY AREA, INC.
1315 Walnut Street, Suite 505
Philadelphia, PA 19107
215/732-2303

Pittsburgh

UNITED MENTAL HEALTH, INC.
401 Wood Street
Pittsburgh, PA 15222
412/391-3820

Pottsville

SCHUYLKILL COUNTY COUNCIL ON
    ALCOHOLISM AND DRUG ABUSE,
    INC.
2nd and Norwegian Streets
P.O. Box 1079
Pottsville, PA 17901

Reading

NCA-BERKS COUNTY, INC.
134 North Fifth Street, 2nd Floor
Reading, PA 19601
215/372-8917

Washington

WASHINGTON COUNTY COUNCIL ON
    ALCOHOLISM & DRUG ABUSE, INC.
87 E. Maiden Street
Washington, PA 15301
412/222-7150
    222-6158

West Chester

CHESTER COUNTY COUNCIL ON
    ADDICTIVE DISEASE, INC.
313 East Lancaster Avenue
Exton East Shops
Exton, PA 19341
215/363-6164

SOUTH CAROLINA

Rock Hill   YORK COUNTY COUNCIL ON
                   ALCOHOL & DRUG ABUSE, INC.
                   P.O. Box 4437CRS
                   103 Sedgewood Drive
                   Rock Hill, SC 29730
                   803/327-3118

SOUTH DAKOTA

State Affiliate

NCA-SOUTH DAKOTA, INC.
101 South Main Street
Suite 505
Sioux Falls, SD 57102
605/331-2554

TENNESSEE

State Affiliate

THE TENNESSEE ASSOCIATION OF ALCOHOL
   & DRUG COUNCILS
1409 Magnolia Avenue
Knoxville, TN 37917
615/546-8666

Jackson   JACKSON AREA COUNCIL ON
                 ALCOHOLISM AND DRUG
                 DEPENDENCY
                 P.O. Box 1867
                 Jackson, TN 38301
                 901/423-3653

Kingsport

KINGSPORT COUNCIL ON
  ALCOHOLISM AND DRUG
  DEPENDENCY
116 E. Market Street
Kingsport, TN 37660
615/245-7281

Nashville

MID-CUMBERLAND COUNCIL ON
  ALCOHOL AND DRUGS, INC.
250 Venture Circle
Metro Center #203
Nashville, TN 37226
615/254-6547

TEXAS

Amarillo

AMARILLO COUNCIL ON
  ALCOHOLISM, INC.
2500 West 8th
Amarillo, TX 79106
806/376-4064

Austin

GREATER AUSTIN COUNCIL ON
  ALCOHOLISM, INC.
608 Morrow Street, Suite 103
Austin, TX 78752
512/454-7627

Houston

HOUSTON REGIONAL COUNCIL ON
  ALCOHOLISM, INC.
3100 West Alabama, Suite 100
Houston, TX 77030
713/520-8582

San Antonio

SAN ANTONIO COUNCIL ON
  ALCOHOLISM, INC.
5307 Broadway, Suite 226
San Antonio, TX 78209
512/828-3742

VIRGINIA

Norfolk

TIDEWATER COUNCIL ON
ALCOHOLISM, INC.
7510 Granby Street, Suite 4
Norfolk, VA 23505
804/588-1495

Winchester

COUNCIL ON ALCOHOLISM/LORD
FAIRFAX COMMUNITY, INC.
315 E. Cork Street
Winchester, VA 22601
703/662-8865/66

VIRGIN ISLANDS

St. Thomas

COUNCIL ON ALCOHOLISM ST.
THOMAS-ST. JOHN
P.O. Box 10028
St. Thomas, U.S.V.I. 00801
809/774-4358

WASHINGTON

State Affiliate

WASHINGTON STATE COUNCIL ON ALCOHOLISM/NCA
360 Bellevue Square, Suite 215
Bellevue, WA 98004
206/454-3413

Bellevue

EASTSIDE ALCOHOL CENTER, INC.
1111–110th Avenue, N.E., Bldg. 400
Bellevue, WA 98004
206/454-1505

Bellingham

WHATCOM COUNTY COMMUNITY
   ALCOHOLISM CENTER
1000 North Forest St.
Bellingham, WA 98225
206/733-1400
   676-6871

Kennewick

BENTON COUNTY COMMUNITY
   ALCOHOLISM CENTER
17 North Cascade
Kennewick, WA 99336
509/586-2161

Kent

SOUTHEAST COMMUNITY ALCOHOL
   CENTER
P.O. Box 1041
232 S. Second
Kent, WA 98031
206/872-3545

Longview

LOWER COLUMBIA COUNCIL ON
   ALCOHOLISM, INC.
835 Fifteenth Avenue
Longview, WA 98632
206/577-2216

Seattle

NORTHEND COMMUNITY ALCOHOL
   CENTER
10501 Meridian Avenue, North
Suite E
Seattle, WA 98133
206/367-2700

Vancouver

CLARK COUNTY COUNCIL ON
   ALCOHOLISM
P.O. Box 1656
Vancouver, WA 98663
206/696-1631

Yakima   COMMUNITY ALCOHOL CENTER
                          102 South Naches Avenue
                          Yakima, WA 98901
                          509/248-1800

WISCONSIN

State Affiliate

WISCONSIN ASSOCIATION ON ALCOHOL
    AND OTHER DRUG ABUSE, INC./NCA
333 West Mifflin Street
Suite 4
Madison, WI 53703
608/257-7970, 71

Kenosha   ALCOHOL AND DRUG COUNCIL OF
                              KENOSHA CO., INC.
                          1202 60th Street (101)
                          Kenosha, WI 53140
                          414/658-8166

La Crosse   COULEE COUNCIL ON ALCOHOLISM
                              & OTHER CHEMICAL ABUSE, INC.
                          921 West Avenue So.
                          La Crosse, WI 54601
                          608/784-4177

Milwaukee   MILWAUKEE COUNCIL ON
                              ALCOHOLISM, INC.
                          2266 North Prospect Avenue
                          Suite 324
                          Milwaukee, WI 53203
                          414/276-8487

Waukesha

WAUKESHA COUNTY COUNCIL ON
ALCOHOLISM & OTHER DRUG
ABUSE, INC.
150 South Street
Waukesha, WI 53186
414/544-4751

West Bend

WASHINGTON COUNTY COUNCIL ON
ALCOHOLISM, INC.
St. Joseph's Community Hospital
551 Silverbrook Drive
P.O. Box 274
West Bend, WI 53095
414/338-1181

INTERNATIONAL DIVISION

Bahamas

BAHAMAS COUNCIL ON
ALCOHOLISM
P.O. Box N-7522
Nassau N.P., Bahamas
Tel: 809-32-21685
     809-32-32026

Bermuda

THE COUNCIL ON ALCOHOLISM
P.O. Box 1673
Hamilton 5, Bermuda
Tel: 2-6796

APPENDIX II

National Association of State Alcohol and Drug Abuse Directors Membership List

Other potential sources of useful information are the men and women connected with state programs on alcoholism and drug abuse. The National Association of State Alcohol and Drug Abuse Directors (NASADAD), with headquarters in Washington, D.C., has courteously made available its membership list, updated to April 1981. The individual names may be outdated but the list should furnish helpful starting points. In the following compilation, (a) means the organization is devoted primarily to alcoholism, (b) means its jurisdiction is drug abuse, and (c) means it is concerned with both. Those emphasizing drug abuse can often be helpful in the field of alcoholism, and vice versa.

Alabama   (c)   Glenn Ireland, II
                     Commissioner
                     Department of Mental Health
                     135 South Union Street
                     Montgomery   36130
                     (205) 834-4350

Alaska   (c)   Robert Cole, Coordinator
                     Dept. of Health & Social Services
                     Office of Alcoholism and Drug Abuse
                     Pouch H-05-F
                     Juneau 99811
                     (907) 586-6201

Arizona   (a)   Alex Arredondo, Manager
                     Alcohol Section
                     AZ Dept. of Health Services
                     2500 East Van Buren
                     Phoenix   85008
                     (602) 255-1239

               (d)   Ed Zborower, Manager
                     Drug Abuse Section
                     Dept. of Health Services
                     Div. of Behavioral Health Services
                     2500 East Van Buren
                     Phoenix   85008
                     (602) 255-1238

Arkansas   (c)   Frankie Wallingsford, Director
                     Arkansas Office on Alcohol and
                         Drug Abuse Prevention
                     1515 W. 7th Avenue, Suite 300
                     Little Rock   72202
                     (501) 371-2603

California   (c)   Sally Davis, Director
                     Dept. of Alcohol and Drug Abuse
                     111 Capitol Mall
                     Sacramento   95814
                     (916) 445-1940 or 322-8484

Colorado   (c)   Herman Diesenhaus, Acting Director
Alcohol and Drug Abuse Division
Department of Health
4210 East 11th Avenue
Denver   80220
(303) 320-6137

Connecticut (c)   Donald J. McConnell, Executive Director
Conn. Alcohol and Drug Abuse Council
999 Asylum Avenue, 3rd Floor
Hartford   06105
(203) 566-4145

Delaware   (c)   William B. Merrill, Chief
Bureau of Alcoholism and Drug Abuse
1901 N. DuPont Highway
Newcastle   19720
(302) 421-6131

District   (c)   Simon Holliday, Chief
of   Alcohol and Drug Abuse
Columbia   Planning Division
601 Indiana Avenue, N.W.
Suite 500
Washington, D.C.   20004
(202) 724-5641

Florida   (a)   Clarence S. Durham, Administrator
Alcoholic Rehabilitation Program
Dept. of Health & Rehabilitation
   Services
1309 Winewood Boulevard, Room 148A
Tallahassee   32301
(904) 487-2820

(d)   Frank D. Nelson, Director
Drug Abuse Program
1309 Winewood Blvd.
Building 6, Room 163A
Tallahassee   32301
(904) 488-0900

Georgia (c) William B. Johnson, Director
Alcohol and Drug Section
Division of Mental Health and
Mental Retardation
GA Dept. of Human Resources
618 Ponce De Leon Avenue, N.E.
Atlanta   30308
(404) 894-4785

Hawaii (d) Denis Mee-Lee, Branch Chief
Alcohol and Drug Abuse Branch
1270 Queen Emma Street, Room 404
Honolulu   96813
(808) 548-7655

Idaho (c) Charles E. Burns, Director
Bureau of Substance Abuse
Department of Health & Welfare
700 West State
Boise   83720
(208) 334-4368

Illinois (a) Mrs. Roalda J. Alderman
Superintendent, Alcohol Division
Ill. Dept. of Mental Health &
Developmental Disabilities
160 North LaSalle Street, Room 1500
Chicago   60601
(312) 793-2907

(d) Thomas B. Kirkpatrick, Jr., Director
Ill. Dangerous Drugs Commission
Suite 1500
Chicago   60601
(312) 822-9860

Indiana (c) John F. Jones, Ass't Commissioner
Division of Addiction Services
Department of Mental Health
429 North Pennsylvania Street
Indianapolis   46204
(317) 232-7816

Iowa   (c)   Gary P. Riedmann, Director
                    Iowa Department of Substance Abuse
                    505 Fifth Avenue
                         Insurance Exchange Building, Suite 202
                    Des Moines   50319
                    (515) 281-3641

Kansas   (c)   Dr. Lorne A. Phillips, Commissioner
                    Alcohol and Drug Abuse Services
                    2700 West Sixth Street
                    Biddle Building
                    Topeka   66606
                    (913) 296-3925

Kentucky   (c)   Michael Townsend, Manager
                    Alcohol and Drug Branch
                    Bureau for Health Services
                    Department of Human Resources
                    275 East Main Street
                    Frankfort   40621
                    (502) 564-2880

Louisiana   (c)   V. Eugene Patrick
                    Office of Mental Health and Substance Abuse
                    P.O. Box 4049
                    655 North 5th Street
                    Baton Rouge   70821
                    (504) 342-2565

Maine   (c)   Michael Fulton, Director
                    Office of Alcoholism and Drug
                         Abuse Prevention
                    Bureau of Rehabilitation
                    32 Winthrop Street
                    Augusta   04330
                    (207) 289-2781

Maryland   (a)   John Bland, Director
                    Alcoholism Control Administration
                    201 West Preston Street, 4th Floor
                    Baltimore   21201
                    (301) 383-2781, 2782, 2783

(d)   Richard L. Hamilton, Director
Maryland State Drug Abuse Administration
201 West Preston Street
Baltimore   21201
(301) 383-3312

Mass   (a)   Edward Blacker, Ph.D., Director
Mass Division of Alcoholism
755 Boylston Street
Boston   02116
(617) 727-1960

(d)   Victor Gelineau, Acting Director
Division of Drug Rehab.
160 N. Washington Street
Boston   02114
(617) 727-8614

Michigan   (c)   Kenneth Eaton, Administrator
Office of Substance Abuse Services
Department of Public Health
3500 North Logan Street
Lansing   48909
(517) 373-8603

Minnesota   (c)   Chuck Heinecke, Director
Chemical Dependency Program Division
Dept. of Public Welfare
4th Floor Centennial Building
658 Cedar
St. Paul   55155
(612) 296-4614

Mississippi   (c)   Anne D. Robertson, Director
Division of Alcohol and Drug Abuse
Department of Mental Health
12th Floor, Robert E. Lee Office Building
Jackson   39201
(601) 354-7031

Missouri	(c)	Ronald Wilson, Director Division of Alcoholism and Drug Abuse Department of Mental Health 2002 Missouri Boulevard P.O. Box 687 Jefferson City 65101 (314) 751-4942
Montana	(c)	Michael Murray, Administrator Alcohol and Drug Abuse Division State of Montana Department of Institutions Helena 59601 (406) 449-2827
Nebraska	(c)	Jim D. Bailey, Director Division on Alcoholism and Drug Abuse Department of Public Institutions P.O. Box 94728 Lincoln 68509 (402) 471-2851, Ext. 415
Nevada	(c)	Richard Ham, Chief Bureau of Alcohol and Drug Abuse Department of Human Resources 505 East King Street Carson City 89710 (702) 885-4790
New Hampshire	(c)	Joseph Diament, Director Office of Alcohol & Drug Abuse Prevention Health and Welfare Building Hazen Drive Concord 03301 (603) 271-4627
New Jersey	(a)	Riley Regan, Director New Jersey Division of Alcoholism 129 East Hanover Street Trenton 08625 (609) 292-8947

       (d)   Richard Russo, MSPH
Director
Division of Narcotic and Drug Abuse Control
129 East Hanover Street
Trenton   08625
(609) 292-5760

New
Mexico   (c)   J. Ronald Vigil, Acting Chief
Substance Abuse Bureau
Behavioral Services Division
Health and Environment Department
P.O. Box 968
Santa Fe   87503
(505) 827-5271, Ext. 228

New
York   (a)   Shelia B. Blume, M.D.
New York Division of Alcoholism
   and Alcohol Abuse
194 Washington Avenue
Albany   12210
(518) 474-5102

       (d)   John S. Gustafson, Ass't.
Division of Substance Abuse Services
Executive Park South
Box 8200
Albany   12203
(518) 457-7629

North
Carolina   (c)   Steven L. Hicks
Deputy Director
Alcohol and Drug Abuse Section
Div. of Mental Health and
   Mental Retardation Services
325 North Salisbury Street
Raleigh   27611
(919) 733-4670

North   (c)   Thomas Hedin, Director
Dakota   Division of Alcoholism & Drug Abuse
                     Mental Health/Mental Retardation Services
                     State Department of Health
                     909 Basin Avenue
                     Bismarck   58505
                     (701) 224-2767

Ohio   (a)   Paul D. Lanham, Chief
                     Division of Alcoholism
                     Ohio Department of Health
                     246 North High Street
                     Columbus   43215
                     (614) 466-3425

               (d)   Joy Holland-Fields, Acting Chief
                     Bureau of Drug Abuse
                     65 South Front Street
                     Columbus   43215
                     (614) 466-9015

Oklahoma   (a)   Tom Stanitis, Director
                     State Alcohol Authority
                     P.O. Box 53277, Capitol Station
                     Oklahoma City   73152
                     (405) 521-2811

               (d)   Glen Wallace, Ed.D., Deputy Director
                     Drug Abuse Services
                     State Dept. of Mental Health
                     P.O. Box 53277, Capitol Station
                     Oklahoma City   73152
                     (405) 521-2811

Oregon   (d)   Jeff Kushner, Assoc. Admin.
                     Mental Health Division
                     2575 Bittern Street, N.E.
                     Salem   97310
                     (503) 378-2163

PA   (c)   Rhea Singsen, Acting Deputy Secretary
                Office of Drug and Alcohol Programs
                Riverside Office, Building No. 1, Suite N
                2101 North Front Street
                Harrisburg   17120
                (717) 787-9857

Rhode   (c)   Richard H. Freeman, Assistant Director
Island   Division of Substance Abuse
                303 General Hospital
                Cranston   02920
                (401) 464-2091

South   (c)   William J. McCord, Director
Carolina   South Carolina Commission on
                   Alcohol and Drug Abuse
                3700 Forest Drive
                Columbia   29204
                (803) 758-2521/2183

South   (a)   John W. Jones, Director
Dakota   South Dakota Div. of Alcoholism
                Joe Foss Building
                Pierre   57501
                (605) 773-4806

          (d)   John W. Jones, Acting Dir.
                Division of Drugs and Substance Control
                Department of Health
                Foss Building
                Pierre   57501
                (605) 773-3123

TN   (c)   Lee Fleisher, Ass't Commissioner
                Alcohol and Drug Abuse Services
                Tennessee Dept. of Mental Health and
                   Mental Retardation
                501 Union Building
                Nashville   37219
                (615) 741-1921

Texas   (a)   Ross Newby, Executive Director
Texas Commission on Alcoholism
809 Sam Houston State Office Bldg.
Austin   78701
(512) 475-2725

         (d)   Newton Key, Director
Drug Abuse Prevention Div.
Texas Dept. of Community Affairs
P.O. Box 13166
Austin   78711
(512) 475-6351

Utah   (c)   Judy Brady, Director
Division of Alcoholism & Drugs
150 West North Temple, Suite 350
P.O. Box 2500
Salt Lake City   84110
(801) 533-6532

Vermont   (c)   Richard Powell III, Acting Director
Alcohol and Drug Abuse Division
103 South Main Street
Waterbury   05676
(802) 241-2170, 241-1000

Virginia   (c)   A. Mort Casson, Ph.D. Assistant
            Commissioner
Division of Substance Abuse
State Dept. of Mental Health
   & Mental Retardation
P.O. Box 1797
109 Governor Street
Richmond   23214
(804) 786-5313

Washington (c)   Glen Miller, Director
Bureau of Alcoholism and Substance Abuse
Washington Dept. of Social & Health Services
Office Building
Olympia   98504
(206) 753-5866

West Virginia	(c)	Raymond E. Washington, Director Division of Alcohol and Drug Abuse State Capitol 1800 Kanawha Boulevard E Charleston 25305 (304) 348-3616
Wisconsin	(c)	Larry W. Monson, ACSW, Director State Bureau of Alcohol and Other Drug Abuse 1 West Wilson Street, P.O. Box 7851 Madison 53707 (608) 266-2717
Wyoming	(c)	Jean DeFratis, Director Alcohol and Drug Abuse Programs Hathaway Building Cheyenne 82002 (307) 777-7115, Ext. 7118
Guam	(c)	Peter A. San Nicolas, Director Mental Health and Substance Abuse Agency Single State Agency Post Office Box 20999 Guam 96921
Puerto Rico	(a)	Ivonne Cordero Muratti Assistant Secretary Puerto Rico Department of Addiction Control Services Box B-Y, Rio Piedras Station Rio Piedras 00928 (809) 763-5014 or 7575
	(d)	Sila Nazario de Ferrer Secretary Department of Addiction Control Services P.O. Box B-Y Piedras Station 00928 (809) 764-8140

Virgin (c) Chester D. Copemann, Ph.D.
Islands   Director, Division of Mental
                Health, Alcoholism and Drug Dependency
             Post Office Box 520
             Christiansted
             St. Croix, Virgin Islands　00820
             (809) 774-4888 dial direct or (809) 249-7959

American (c) Jan King
Samoa   Program Director
              Department of Mental Health Clinic
              LBJ Tropical Medical Center
              Pago, Pago, American Samoa　96799

              William Walkers, Director
              Mental Health Clinic
              Pago Pago

Trust   (c) Masao Kumangai, M.D., Director
Territories   Health Services
               Office of the High Commissioner
               Saipan　96950